GRAMMAR
SUCCESS
IN 20 MINUTES
A DAY

GRAMMAR SUCCESS
IN 20 MINUTES
A DAY

LEARNINGEXPRESS®

NEW YORK

Library of Congress Cataloging-in-Publication Data:
   Grammar success : in 20 minutes a day.
      p. cm.
   ISBN: 978-1-57685-600-0
   1. English language—Grammar—Problems, exercises, etc. I. LearningExpress (Organization)

PE1112.G676 2008

428.2—dc22

                                                    2007038881

Printed in the United States of America

9 8 7 6 5 4 3 2 1

ISBN: 978-1-57685-600-0

For information on LearningExpress, other LearningExpress products, or bulk sales, please write to us at:
   LearningExpress
   55 Broadway
   8th Floor
   New York, NY 10006

Or visit us at:
   www.learnatest.com

Contents

CONTENTS

Introduction ▶

Do your grammar skills need some brushing up? Perhaps you have an exam on your horizon, or you want to hone your grammar skills to help improve your writing or speech. Whatever the case may be, this quick reference guide will help put you well on your way toward accomplishing your grammar goals—no matter how big or small.

Because English is so complex, the rules and guidelines—called grammar and usage—are necessary to help us better understand its many idiosyncrasies. While language is forever changing to meet our needs, the inner workings of a sentence are, for the most part, as constant as the stars, and figuring out these dynamics is like putting a puzzle together (or taking it apart, if you will). Understanding the inner workings of a sentence will ultimately help you with your speech and writing—the essence of communication and language. And the benefits of your efforts will always far outweigh the loss of about 20 or so minutes of your day.

Before you begin to progress through the book, take the time to determine what you know and what you might need to focus more on by taking the pretest. You might be surprised just how much you remember!

Pretest

Before you start your study of grammar skills, you may want to get an idea of how much you already know and how much you need to learn. If that's the case, take the pretest that follows.

The pretest consists of 50 multiple-choice questions covering all the lessons in this book. Naturally, 50 questions can't cover every single concept or rule you will learn by working through these pages. So even if you answer all of the questions on the pretest correctly, it's almost guaranteed that you will find a few ideas or rules in this book that you didn't already know. On the other hand, if you get a lot of the answers wrong on this pretest, don't despair. This book will show you how to improve your grammar and writing, step by step.

So use this pretest for a general idea of how much of what's in this book you already know. If you get a high score, you may be able to spend less time with this book than you originally planned. If you get a low score, you may find that you will need more than 20 minutes a day to get through each chapter and learn all the grammar and mechanics concepts you need.

Record the answers in this book. If the book doesn't belong to you, write the numbers 1–50 on a piece of paper and write your answers there. Take as much time as you need to complete this short test. When you finish, check your answers against the answer section that follows. Each answer tells you which lesson of this book teaches you about the grammatical rule in that question.

▶ Pretest

1. Circle the common nouns.

soda	love	puppy
Jamaica	thoughtlessness	Logan Road
troubling	clapping	zip
friendly	sorrow	mend

2. Circle the abstract nouns.

peace	telephone	livelihood
deceit	cheerfulness	jungle
NASA	smile	rubber band
test	eyelash	patience

3. Circle the proper nouns.

Texas	Work	Clock
Puzzle	Nancy	Mr. Klondike
Licorice	Mexico City	Basketball
IBM	Spiderman	Mt. Everest

4. Circle the nouns that are pluralized correctly.

stockings	partys	deer
knots	tooths	cacti
chimnies	mice	radioes
dresses	guies	suitcases

5. Circle the hyphenated nouns that are spelled correctly.

sister-in-laws	kilowatt-hours
runner-ups	forget-me-nots
follow-ups	sticks-in-the-mud

6. Circle the nouns that have been correctly made possessive.

child's	her's	Jody's
Congress'	tooth's	cactus's
puppies'	moms'	Jason's
women's	his'	dress's

7. Circle the antecedents/pronouns that properly agree in gender.

John/he	bird/she
fish/his	Mrs. Brown/she
student/it	Mr. Cho/her

8. Circle the antecedents/pronouns that agree in number.

kids/him	everybody/they
Kathy and I/it	fish/they
group/it	fish/it
each/he or she	woman/we
both/they	

9. Circle the interrogative pronouns.

who	when	whose
which	whom	whomever
how	where	what

10. Circle the subjective case pronouns.

I went to his house and saw him.

She brought me an apple and I thanked her.

They went to Pat's and called me.

11. Circle the objective case pronouns.

He threw it toward me.

Pass me the salt.

We made them sandwiches.

12. Circle the reflexive case pronouns and underline the possessive case pronouns.

She helped herself to the apple pie her mom made this afternoon.

Drew's headache was so bad he couldn't bring himself to finish paying his bills.

We ourselves are responsible for our own happiness.

13. Circle the demonstrative pronouns and underline the relative pronouns.

That is the most annoying sound that I have ever heard.

Those are the boxes of blankets that Mom plans to take to the SPCA.

Is this the channel that you were watching?

14. Circle the action verbs.

wash	be	hold	cook
would	buy	pray	gnaw
put	write	loan	marry

15. Circle the linking verbs.

appear	took	become	sat
feel	prove	call	grow
study	look	is	lose

16. Circle the regular verbs and underline the irregular verbs.

forgive	grow	buy	walk
wash	hide	sew	pet
sit	hear	play	throw

17. Circle the correct form of lay/lie in each sentence.

Joy found her hairbrush (laying, lying) in the suitcase.

The swing has (lain, laid) broken behind the shed for two years.

The boy had (laid, lain) awake before getting up to play.

18. Circle the correct form of sit/set in each sentence.

The class (set, sat) patiently as the teacher took attendance.

Claudia's aunt (sits, sets) the table while Gert cooks dinner.

(Setting, Sitting) on the porch on a cool summer night is the best.

19. Circle the correct tricky verb in each sentence.

Sandy carefully (hanged, hung) her new curtains on the window.

Peter tried to (accept, except) his explanation, but it was difficult.

You (can, may) take another glass of lemonade if you like.

20. Identify the tense of the verbs that follow as: present, past, future, present perfect, past perfect, future perfect, present progressive, past progressive, or future progressive.

will drive	am driving
had driven	drove
drive	has driven
drives	will have driven

21. Circle the common adjectives in the following sentences.

Dan went to the community library to research the American Revolution.

The beach is the perfect place to relax and read a good book.

Ben was sad that his new radio had broken.

22. Place the correct indefinite article in front of each noun.

___ house	___ elephant
___ unicorn	___ yellow flower
___ one-way street	___ honor
___ underdog	___ loafer
___ unopened gift	___ orange
___ hour	___ occasion
___ wrist	___ admirer
___ upper level	

23. Change the following proper nouns into proper adjectives.

Italy	Bahama	Africa
Texas	France	Hawaii
America	Virginia	Denmark
California	Belgium	China
Japan	Inca	England

24. Determine whether the boldfaced word in each sentence is a possessive pronoun or a possessive adjective.

> **His** sneakers were worn, so he bought new ones.
>
> Marissa crossed **her** fingers and hoped the winning ticket would be **hers**.
>
> **My** uncle showed me an autographed Babe Ruth baseball card and said it would one day be mine.

25. Determine whether the boldfaced word in each sentence is a demonstrative pronoun or a demonstrative adjective.

> **This** is really over-the-top!
>
> Take **this** money and buy yourself a treat.
>
> Watch **these** carefully while they boil.

26. Determine which form of comparative or superlative adjective best completes each sentence.

> Terry's (most high, highest) jump in the high jump was four feet, six inches.
>
> Sean's bank account was (larger, more large) than mine.
>
> Barbara was (best, better) at chess than her roommate Natalie.

27. Circle the correct form of the comparative and superlative adverbs in the following sentences.

> Joel was (less, least) active during the winter than during the summer.
>
> The store brand's price was the (low, lower, lowest) of the three brands.
>
> This was the (long, longer, longest) day of the year.

28. Determine whether the boldfaced word in the sentence is an adjective or an adverb.

> The accounting department ran at a **fast** but friendly pace.
>
> Cory worked **hard** on improving his tennis swing for the tournament.
>
> Nora was sent **straight** to her room for disobeying her parents.

29. Identify the prepositional phrases in the following sentences.

> Ferdinand Magellan was the first explorer to sail around the world.
>
> Without a doubt, regular exercise is necessary for good health.
>
> The little monkey ran around Mom's living room and climbed up the drapes.

30. Determine whether the boldfaced word is a preposition or an adverb.

> Holly was **beside** herself with fear when the child darted into the street.
>
> If we can reach Hightstown **by** five, we may be able to see the president's motorcade go **by**.
>
> Use caution when you walk **across** busy streets.

31. Rewrite each sentence so that the misplaced modifiers are properly placed.

> The woman was walking her dog with hair curlers.
>
> Walking along the shore the sand burned my feet.
>
> Tina bought a guinea pig for her brother they call Butterscotch.

32. Using the clues, write the homonyms or homographs.

school leader/integrity

to crack/a short rest

carry on/curriculum vitae

rip/saline from the eye

good/underwater spring

wrapped/a boo-boo

33. Identify the simple subject in the following sentences.

Next week, Scott and Jennifer will get married.

Shopping sprees can be fun, but very expensive.

It may be too soon to tell.

34. Identify the simple predicate in the following sentences.

Reading is good exercise for the brain.

Try again.

The log, when turned over, revealed a whole different world.

35. Identify whether the boldfaced word is a direct or an indirect object in the following sentences.

Brandy took the **pot** of flowers and brought **it** into the garden window.

Grumbling to himself, Stan dragged the heavy **garbage cans** out to the street.

He gave **her** a **high-five** to assure her that all was well.

36. Identify the verb that correctly agrees with the subject in each sentence.

Patty (fly, flies) frequently for work.

All of us (watch, watches) out for one another.

Nobody (want, wants) to play croquet in the the backyard with me.

37. Identify the verb that correctly completes the following sentences.

Neither Jessica nor Marty (like, likes) to do the laundry.

Spaghetti and meatballs (is, are) my favorite Italian meal.

Sally or Zach (is, are) probably going to be the valedictorian this year.

38. Identify the verb that will agree with the indefinite pronouns in the following sentences.

Everything (go, goes) to the basement for sorting.

Somebody (need, needs) to bring some milk home.

While others (prefers, prefer) to eat salad first, I prefer to eat it last.

39. Determine which pronoun best fits for proper pronoun/antecedent agreement in each sentence.

The boys took _____ time walking home from school.

Nobody saw _____ name on the cast list.

The scared joey hopped to _____ mother for security.

40. Identify the adjective and adverb phrases in the following sentences.

Books with weak spines need to be reinforced to lengthen their shelf life.

The lizard scurried across the sidewalk and disappeared into the bushes.

The cashier with the red hair and braces was especially helpful.

41. Identify the participial phrases, infinitive phrases, and gerund phrases in the following sentences.

Hoping to win the lottery, Harriet bought 50 tickets for tonight's drawing.

To help pass the time, Jake reads a book that he takes along.

Caring for her ailing grandmother is Lori's focus right now.

42. Identify the appositive phrases in the following sentences.

Ron, a referee and mentor, is a fair-minded and friendly man.

Jeannine works for KTL, a telecommunications company in Kansas City.

Molly, my student, has a very fanciful imagination.

43. Determine whether each group of words is an independent or a subordinate clause.

Made to order

Loosen up a little bit

Don't make any assumptions

We'll just see about that

Before you go

Have a nice day

44. Identify the adjective clause in each sentence.

Now I remember the guy that you described to me yesterday.

The house at the end of the road is where my father grew up.

The room next to the office is where the professors meet.

45. Identify the noun clause in each sentence.

I can see what you mean.

What Wendy said took everyone by surprise.

How it ends remains to be seen.

46. Identify the adverb clause in each sentence.

Because it was getting late, Sonya got her things ready to go.

It will be an enjoyable gathering, provided it doesn't rain.

Craig was going to try to reach the finish line, even though it seemed so far off.

47. Identify the coordinating conjunction(s) in each sentence, and the word or group of words it is connecting.

Logan or Melanie can go to the retreat if they want to.

Karla wanted to visit longer with her friend, but she had a long drive home and it was late.

We signed up for the early class so we could have the rest of the afternoon free.

48. Identify the simple, compound, complex, and compound-complex sentences.
   a. We can go to dinner now or we can go after the concert.
   b. When the judge announced the winner, the audience clapped loudly and gave him a standing ovation.
   c. All of the graduates will receive a degree.
   d. If you try harder, you will certainly achieve success.

49. Add punctuation where necessary in the following sentences.

Nathans birthday is May 21 1991 which fell on a Monday this year

Mr Roberts left a message asking me to pick up these items staples printer paper correction fluid and two boxes of paper clips I guess the supply closet got raided

All of the girls dresses were pink with white eyelet ruffles on the sleeves edges.

50. Correctly place quotation marks, commas, and end marks in the following sentences.

Are we almost there yet Jodi asked for the ninth time.

And if you look to your left the tour guide went on to say you'll see Elvis's home, Graceland

▶ Answers

If you miss any of the following questions, you may refer to the designated lesson for further explanation.

1. soda, love, puppy, thoughtlessness, clapping, sorrow (Lesson 1)

2. peace, livelihood, deceit, cheerfulness, patience (Lesson 1)

3. Texas, Nancy, Mr. Klondike, Mexico City, IBM, Spiderman, Mt. Everest (Lesson 1)

4. stockings, deer, knots, cacti, mice, dresses, suitcases (Lesson 2)

5. kilowatt-hours, forget-me-nots, follow-ups, sticks-in-the-mud (Lesson 2)

6. child's, Jody's, Congress', tooth's, cactus's, puppies', moms', Jason's, women's, dress's (Lesson 2)

7. John/he, Mrs. Brown/she (Lesson 3)

8. fish/they, group/it, fish/it, each/he or she, both/they (Lesson 3)

9. who, whose, which, whom, whomever (Lesson 3)

10. (I) went to his house and saw him.
    (She) brought me an apple and (I) thanked her.
    (They) went to Pat's and called me.
    (Lesson 3)

11. He threw (it) toward (me).
    Pass (me) the salt.
    We made (them) sandwiches.
    (Lesson 3)

12. She helped (herself) to the apple pie **her** mom made this afternoon.
    Drew's headache was so bad he couldn't bring (himself) to finish paying **his** bills.
    We (ourselves) are responsible for **our** own happiness.
    (Lesson 3)

13. (That) is the most annoying sound **that** I have ever heard.
    (Those) are the boxes of blankets **that** Mom plans to take to the SPCA.
    Is (this) the channel **that** you were watching?
    (Lesson 3)

14. wash, hold, cook, buy, pray, gnaw, put, write, loan, marry (Lesson 4)

15. appear, become, feel, prove, grow, look (Lesson 4)

16. forgive   grow   buy   (walk)
    (wash)   hide   sew   pet
    sit   hear   (play)   throw
    (Lesson 5)

17. lying, lain, lain (Lesson 5)

18. sat, sets, Sitting (Lesson 5)

19. hung, accept, may (Lesson 5)

20. will drive: future
    had driven: past perfect
    drive: present
    drives: present
    am driving: present progressive
    drove: past
    has driven: present perfect
    will have driven: future perfect
    (Lesson 6)

21. community, perfect, good, new (Lesson 7)

22. a house, a unicorn, a one-way street, an underdog, an unopened gift, an hour, a wrist, an upper level, an elephant, a yellow flower, an honor, a loafer, an orange, an occasion, an admirer
    (Lesson 7)

23. Italian, Bahamian, African, Texan, French, Hawaiian, American, Virginian, Danish, Californian, Belgian, Chinese, Japanese, Incan, English
    (Lesson 7)

24. **His**: possessive adjective; **her**: possessive adjective; **hers**: possessive pronoun; **My**: possessive adjective (Lesson 7)

25. **This**: demonstrative pronoun; **this**: demonstrative adjective; **these**: demonstrative pronoun (Lesson 7)

26. highest, larger, better (Lesson 7)

27. less, lowest, longest (Lesson 8)

28. fast: adjective; **hard:** adverb; **straight:** adverb
(Lessons 7 and 8)

29. around the world; Without a doubt; for good health; around Mom's living room; up the drapes (Lesson 9)

30. beside herself: preposition; **by** five: preposition; **by:** adverb; **across** busy streets: preposition (Lesson 9)

31. The woman with hair curlers was walking her dog.
The sand burned my feet while I was walking along the shore.
Tina bought a guinea pig they call Butterscotch for her brother.
(Lesson 10)

32. principal/principle   tear/tear
break/break   well/well
resume/resume   wound/wound
(Lesson 10)

33. Scott and Jennifer; Shopping sprees; It (Lesson 11)

34. is; Try; revealed (Lesson 11)

35. pot: direct object; **it:** direct object; **garbage cans:** direct object; **her:** indirect object; **high-five:** direct object (Lesson 11)

36. flies, watch, wants (Lesson 12)

37. likes, is, is (Lesson 12)

38. goes, needs, prefer (Lesson 12)

39. their, his or her, its (Lesson 12)

40. with weak spines: adjective phrase
across the sidewalk: adverb phrase; into the bushes: adverb phrase
with the red hair and braces: adjective phrase
(Lesson 13)

41. Hoping to win the lottery: participial phrase
To help pass the time: infinitive phrase
Caring for her ailing grandmother: gerund phrase
(Lesson 13)

42. a referee and mentor
a telecommunications company in Kansas City
my student
(Lesson 13)

43. Made to order: subordinate clause
Loosen up a little bit: independent clause
Don't make any assumptions: independent clause
We'll just see about that: independent clause
Before you go: subordinate clause
Have a nice day: independent clause
(Lesson 14)

44. that you described
where my father grew up
where the professors meet
(Lesson 14)

45. what you mean
What Wendy said
How it ends
(Lesson 14)

46. Because it was getting late
provided it doesn't rain
even though it seemed so far off
(Lesson 14)

47. Logan **or** Melanie
Karla wanted to visit longer with her friend, **but** she had a long drive home **and** it was late.
We signed up for the early class **so** we could have the rest of the afternoon free.
(Lesson 15)

48. a. compound; **b.** compound-complex; **c.** simple; **d.** complex
(Lesson 16)

49. Nathan's birthday is May 21, 1991, which fell on a Monday this year.
Mr. Roberts left a message asking me to pick up these items: staples, printer paper, correction fluid, and two boxes of paper clips; I guess the supply closet got raided.
All of the girls' dresses were pink with white eyelet ruffles on the sleeves' edges.
(Lessons 17–20)

50. "Are we almost there yet?" Jodi asked for the ninth time.
"And if you look to your left," the tour guide went on to say, "you'll see Elvis's home, Graceland."
(Lessons 17–20)

Nouns and Pronouns

1 ▶ Kinds of Nouns

LESSON SUMMARY

Learn why the noun, and its six identifiable subgroups, is the fundamental component of our language.

**ouns**, the most basic component of a language, are naming words. We can break nouns into six identifiable groups: common nouns, proper nouns, concrete nouns, abstract nouns, collective nouns, and compound nouns. It's useful to know about nouns and their important place in the context of writing and grammar—even in speaking, if it's to be done correctly—as so many other parts of speech relate to them in some form. So, here is where we'll begin.

The following table briefly summarizes the six noun groups and the unique qualities that separate them from one another. We will look at them in more detail later.

▶ The Six Types of Nouns

Common Nouns

A **common noun** is a word that speaks of something only in a general way, like *book, car,* and *person.* Common nouns can be written in singular form (*book, car,* and *person*) or plural (*books, cars,* and *people*).

Proper Nouns

Unlike common nouns, **proper nouns** name a very specific person, place, or thing. One distinguishing aspect of proper nouns is that they *always* begin with a capital letter. *Catcher in the Rye, BMW Z4,* and *Arnold Schwarzenegger* are proper nouns.

Concrete Nouns

Concrete nouns name something that appeals to your senses. For instance, *toothbrush, cell phone, moonlight, waves,* and *breezes* are all concrete nouns.

Abstract Nouns

Abstract nouns name beliefs, concepts, and characteristics or qualities—things that can't be touched, seen, or accrued. For example, *composure, sovereignty, free enterprise, daring,* and *handsome* are abstract.

Collective Nouns

Collective nouns are words used to name people, places, and things in terms of a unit. For instance, *class, flock, herd,* and *family* are collective nouns.

Compound Nouns

New words can be formed by combining two or more words, thus forming a compound word. Compounds can be made up of a number of speech components, including nouns, verbs, adjectives, and adverbs. Some examples of compounds are *motorcycle, onlooker, input, software,* and *washing machine.*

▶ A Closer Look at Nouns

Proper nouns are easily distinguishable from common nouns by their capital letters. But be cautious. Don't assume that every word in a sentence that begins with a capital is a proper noun. Basic sentence structure dictates that every sentence must begin with a capital letter—remember that from some distant English class? Also, what might appear to be a proper noun, or some form thereof, could instead be a proper adjective simply because it is describing or telling about a noun that follows it in the sentence. For example, the proper noun *Florida* is acting as a proper adjective in the following sentence because it is used to describe the word *sunshine.*

> **Example:**
> Almost nothing beats the warmth of Florida sunshine.

In the following sentence, *Florida* is a proper noun, because it is not describing another word

> **Example:**
> My family goes to Florida every summer for vacation.

EXAMPLES OF PROPER NOUNS BY CATEGORY	
PEOPLE	
Officials	President G.W. Bush, Mayor Giuliani, Officer Dunlap
Historic Figures	Benjamin Franklin, Cleopatra, Lewis and Clark
Actors	Audrey Hepburn, James Stewart, Lucille Ball
Authors	Jack London, Shakespeare, O. Henry
Artists	Picasso, Vincent van Gogh, Rembrandt
PLACES	
States	Oklahoma, Michigan, New Jersey
Restaurants	Olive Garden, Red Lobster, Salt Creek Grille
Structures	Eiffel Tower, Washington Monument, Empire State Building
Universities	Penn State University, Princeton University, Monmouth University
THINGS	
Transportation	Delta Airlines, Greyhound, Amtrak
Businesses	FedEx, Toys "R" Us, Barnes and Noble
Products	Hebrew National hot dogs, Microsoft Word, Pantene shampoo

Practice

Determine whether the boldfaced words are proper nouns or proper adjectives in the following sentences.

1. The movie *Gone with the Wind* is a classic, wouldn't you agree?

2. **University of Richmond**, like most colleges, holds open house sessions throughout the summer.

3. This **UPS** tracking code seems to have expired.

4. Every **November**, he trades his **Jeep** in for a newer model.

5. The **Smithsonian Institute** comprises more than 19 museums in the nation's capital of **Washington, D.C.**

6. A **Degas** painting once sold for over four million dollars at **Sotheby's**, an auction house in **London**.

7. You can see for miles from the observation deck of the **Sears Tower** in **Chicago, Illinois**.

8. The **French** toast was exceptionally delicious at breakfast this morning.

9. The **French** toast the **New Year** with the phrase "bonne année!"

Concrete nouns are fairly simple to identify. They are nouns that appeal to your senses—hearing, touch, taste, smell, and sight. Besides things like an *avalanche*, a *stretch limo*, *newborn kittens*, or a piping hot plate of *barbeque ribs*, things such as *air*, *cells*, *molecules*, and *atoms* are concrete, even though they can't readily be seen with the naked eye. Got the idea?

Abstract nouns, on the other hand, name ideas, qualities or characteristics, and feelings. Words such as *pride*, *resentfulness*, *health*, *democracy*, and *love* fall into this category. Do you see the difference between the two?

Practice

Identify the boldfaced nouns as either concrete or abstract in the following sentences.

10. The caring **message** written in my get-well **card** was **evidence** of Kim's **thoughtfulness** and **compassion**.

11. The **globalization** of **capitalism** has become tremendous in the last **quarter-century** due to improved **technology**.

12. There's a lot to be said for the age-old **adage** "**Beauty** is in the **eye** of the **beholder**."

13. His **intuition** told **him** to swerve right in order to avoid the potential **accident**.

Take a look at a list of collective nouns, and you're sure to get a few chuckles. Some are fairly familiar, such as *herd*, *club*, *family*, and *committee*. But did you know that a group of oysters is called a *bed*? That a group of butterflies is called a *kaleidoscope*? That a group of islands is called a *chain*? Or that a group of ships is called a *flotilla*?

A collective noun can take either a singular or a plural verb, depending on how it is used in the sentence. Take the word *choir*, for instance. In the sentence

> The choir travels to out-of-state performances by bus.

the *choir* is taken as a single unit and therefore takes the singular verb (*the collective group travels*). The follow-

ing sentence, on the other hand, uses the word *choir* in a plural sense.

> The choir are fitted for new robes every three years.

This implies that all the individual choir members are fitted for new robes every three years. While the sentence may sound odd, this must obviously be the case, as *each* individual member wears a robe; the *group* as a single unit doesn't wear a robe.

Practice

Identify the correct verb or pronoun for each collective noun in the following sentences.

14. A dozen roses (is, are) a thoughtful gift for Valentine's Day.

15. A dozen students (is, are) going to the library to study for finals.

16. The class took (its, their) yearly field trip to Camp Arrowhead this past April.

17. The class completed (its, their) exam in American History and did very well.

18. The committee submitted (its, their) findings on the case to the jury.

19. The committee took (its, their) seat(s) to hear the verdict.

Compound nouns present many writers with issues regarding spelling, rather than usage. There are three ways to spell these nouns, which are made up of two or more words. The closed form refers to two words joined without any space between them, such as *bandwagon*, *forthwith*, and *skyscraper*. The open form has a space between the words, like *water ski* and *stainless steel*. The hyphenated form uses hyphens (-) between the words, like *well-to-do* and *drought-stricken*.

Be careful to distinguish between words that have different meanings as a word pair and as a compound word. The following table lists a few of the most commonly confused compound words.

WORD PAIR	MEANING	COMPOUND WORD	MEANING
all ready	completely prepared	*already*	it happened
all together	as a group	*altogether*	completely
every one	each individual	*everyone*	everybody

Practice

Can you identify the six types of verbs in the following sentences? Identify the boldfaced nouns as common, proper, concrete, abstract, collective, or compound. Some nouns may fit into more than one of these categories.

20. Place the **stamp** on the upper right-hand **corner** of the **envelope** addressed to **Phillip Ware**.

21. It seemed as though the long and brutal **snowstorm** was starting to give way, and some **peace** was going to finally ensue.

22. The **army** of **ants** attacked the defenseless **caterpillar** on my front **sidewalk**.

23. **Tristan** carried a **deck** of cards with him to pass the **time** in between **performances**.

▶ Answers

1. proper noun
2. proper noun
3. proper adjective (*UPS* is modifying *tracking code*)
4. proper noun, proper noun
5. proper noun, proper noun
6. proper adjective (*Degas* is modifying *painting*), proper noun, proper noun
7. proper noun, proper noun
8. proper adjective (*French* is modifying *toast*)
9. proper noun (here, *French* is a proper noun meaning *people from France*, and *toast* is a verb), proper noun
10. concrete, concrete, concrete, abstract, abstract
11. abstract, abstract, concrete, abstract
12. concrete, abstract, concrete, concrete
13. abstract, concrete, concrete
14. is
15. are
16. its
17. their
18. its
19. their
20. **stamp:** common, concrete; **corner:** common, concrete; **envelope:** common, concrete; **Phillip Ware:** proper
21. **snowstorm:** common, concrete; **peace:** common, abstract
22. **army:** common, concrete, collective; **ants:** common, concrete; **caterpillar:** common, concrete; **sidewalk:** common, concrete, compound
23. **Tristan:** proper; **deck:** common, concrete, collective; **time:** common, abstract; **performances:** common, concrete

L E S S O N

2 ▶ Noun Usage

LESSON SUMMARY

Pluralize singular nouns, and turn them into possessives with ease—spelling tips included.

▶ Plurals

Most, but not all, nouns can be made plural by simply adding an *-s* or *-es* at the end of the word, like printer/printer*s*, lunch/lunch*es*, bill/bill*s*, etc. Some nouns, however, actually change their word form altogether, while others don't change at all. Here are some important rules for making a singular noun plural.

MAKING SINGULAR NOUNS PLURAL

1. Add *-s* to the end of most words to make them plural.

grill/grills, paper/papers, snake/snakes, razor/razors

The plural form of nouns like these, referred to as *count nouns*, is rather predictable.

2. Add *-es* to the end of words ending with *-ch, -s, -sh, -ss, -x,* and *-z*.

punch/punches, gas/gases, garlic press/garlic presses, brush/brushes, box/boxes, fez/fezes

It would be strange to try and pronounce dresss or crashs if we didn't put an *e* in front of the *s*, which forms another syllable.

3. Change *-f, -lf,* or *-fe* at the end of words to *-ves*.

leaf/leaves, half/halves, knife/knives

Be careful; there are exceptions to this rule, for example, chief/chiefs, giraffe/giraffes.

4. Change *-y* to *-ies* when the *-y* follows a consonant.

party/parties, battery/batteries, penny/pennies, baby/babies

5. Just add an *-s* after a *-y* when the *-y* is preceded by a vowel.

guy/guys, day/days, play/plays, key/keys, boy/boys

6. Add *-es* to words ending with an *-o* that follows a consonant.

tornado/tornadoes, potato/potatoes, echo/echoes, hero/heroes

7. Simply add *-s* to words ending with an *-o* that follows another vowel.

patio/patios, video/videos, radio/radios

Be careful; there are exceptions to this rule. For example, banjo/banjos, piano/pianos

8. For hyphenated compound nouns, add an *-s* to the word that is changing in number.

passer-by/passers-by, brother-in-law/brothers-in-law

9. There are no rules for pluralizing irregular nouns; you must memorize them.

mice/mouse, deer/deer, child/children, man/men, foot/feet, person/people, stimulus/stimuli, tooth/teeth, octopus/octopi, die/dice, louse/lice, ox/oxen

Practice

Decide whether to add *-s* or *-es* to the end of each word in order to make it plural.

1. book

2. strength

3. bush

4. box

5. package

6. choice

7. edge

8. freedom

9. ogre

10. fox

11. pencil

12. ax

Identify the correct plural for each of the boldfaced words.

13. half	→	halves	halfs
14. chief	→	chieves	chiefs
15. life	→	lifes	lives
16. giraffe	→	giraffes	giraves
17. oaf	→	oafs	oaves
18. shelf	→	shelves	shelfs
19. sniff	→	sniffs	snives
20. wife	→	wives	wifes
21. safe	→	safes	saves
22. wolf	→	wolves	wolfs
23. monkey	→	monkies	monkeys
24. library	→	librarys	libraries
25. candy	→	candies	candys
26. story	→	storys	stories
27. chimney	→	chimneys	chimnies
28. essay	→	essays	essaies
29. daisy	→	daisys	daisies
30. alley	→	alleys	allies
31. delay	→	delaies	delays
32. family	→	families	familys

33. domino	→	dominoes	dominos
34. radio	→	radioes	radios
35. volcano	→	volcanos	volcanoes
36. tomato	→	tomatoes	tomatos
37. torpedo	→	torpedos	torpedoes
38. hero	→	heroes	heros
39. echo	→	echos	echoes
40. piano	→	pianoes	pianos
41. mosquito	→	mosquitoes	mosquitos
42. silo	→	siloes	silos
43. studio	→	studios	studioes
44. six-year-old	→	sixes-year-old	six-year-olds
45. go-between	→	goes-between	go-betweens
46. editor-in-chief	→	editors-in-chief	editor-in-chiefs
47. runner-up	→	runners-up	runner-ups
48. great-grandmother	→	greats-grandmother	great-grandmothers
49. singer-songwriter	→	singers-songwriter	singer-songwriters
50. sister-in-law	→	sister-in-laws	sisters-in-law
51. city-state	→	cities-state	city-states
52. deer	→	deers	deer
53. woman	→	womans	women

54. goose	→	geese	gooses
55. child	→	childs	children
56. moose	→	mooses	moose
57. mouse	→	mice	mouses
58. alumnus	→	alumnuses	alumni
59. phenomenon	→	phenomena	phenomenons
60. cactus	→	cactuses	cacti
61. analysis	→	analysises	analyses
62. criterion	→	criterias	criteria

▶ Possessives

Possessive nouns are words that imply ownership—something belonging to something else. The important thing is first of all to determine whether the word being used actually implies possession.

Singular Possessives

Take the sentence *the bird nests had eggs inside.* The word *nests*, while it ends with an *-s*, is plural, not possessive. To make *nest* or any singular noun possessive, add an apostrophe and an *-s* (*'s*) to the end of the word, as in *child/child's*, *bread/bread's*, or *music/music's*.

> **Example:**
> The *child's* older sister was my *neighbor's friend's* babysitter.

What this sentence tells us is that the older sister of the child was the babysitter of the friend of my neighbor. In other words, the sister "belonged" to the child, the friend "belonged" to the neighbor, and the neighbor "belonged" to me.

Practice
Write the possessive form of the phrases below.

63. the desk of the secretary

64. the applause of the crowd

65. the birthday of Heather

66. the front door of the house

67. the ball glove of Matt

Plural Possessives

Making a plural noun possessive is a bit different. Most plural nouns end with an *-s*, except for irregular nouns (see page 24) like *mouse/mice*, *child/children*, *man/men*, *deer/deer*, and so on. In the case of a regular noun, simply add an apostrophe *after* the *-s* (*s'*), as in *girls/girls'*, *schools/schools'*, or *newspapers/newspapers'*.

> **Example:**
> The *districts' administrators' secretaries'* contracts were approved.

This sentence tells us that the contracts of the secretaries of the administrators of the district were approved. In other words, the administrators "belonged" to the district, the secretaries "belonged" to the administrators, and the contracts "belonged" to the secretaries.

Irregular nouns, such as *teeth* or *people*, are treated like singular nouns, and *'s* is added to them to form a possessive.

Example:
> The geese's V formation in the sky was impressive as they flew overhead.

Practice

Write the possessive form of the phrases below.

68. the dictionaries of the writers

69. the calendars of the doctors

70. the hills of ants

71. the islands of the countries

72. the formations of the geese

When you are confronted with a singular noun ending in *-s*, and you need to make it possessive, you can do one of two things: add an *'s* or add an apostrophe after the *-s*.

Examples:
> **Tess's** new shoes hurt her feet, but she wore them anyway.
> **Tess'** new shoes hurt her feet, but she wore them anyway.

Some words will *sound* awkward with the added *s* at the end (*Moses's*, *Dickens's*, *Williams's*, etc.). It is recommended that you simply add an apostrophe after the *-s* at the end of these names, but the matter is left to your discretion.

Plurals Formed with *'s*

What's a rule without an exception? There are a few instances where you may need to use apostrophe *s* (*'s*) to make a plural. For example, you should add an *'s* to pluralize an abbreviation that has more than one period, such as *Ph.D.* or *M.D.*

Example:
> M.D.'s and Ph.D.'s denote doctorates in medicine and philosophy.

Also, when you need to write an expression with words and letters that are usually not seen in the plural form—like *if*, *and*, or *but*, or *P* and *Q*—you should add *'s* to the word or letter.

Example:
> There are no if's, and's, or but's about it, she won't be going to the concert tomorrow. She should have minded her P's and Q's and kept her comments to herself.

▶ Answers

1. book*s*
2. strength*s*
3. bush*es*
4. box*es*
5. package*s*
6. choice*s*
7. edge*s*
8. freedom*s*
9. ogre*s*
10. fox*es*
11. pencil*s*
12. ax*es*
13. halves
14. chiefs
15. lives
16. giraffes
17. oafs
18. shelves
19. sniffs
20. wives
21. safes
22. wolves
23. monkeys
24. libraries
25. candies
26. stories
27. chimneys
28. essays
29. daisies
30. alleys
31. delays
32. families
33. dominoes
34. radios
35. volcanoes
36. tomatoes

37. torpedoes
38. heroes
39. echoes
40. pianos
41. mosquitoes
42. silos
43. studios
44. six-year-olds
45. go-betweens
46. editors-in-chief
47. runners-up
48. great-grandmothers
49. singer-songwriters
50. sisters-in-law
51. city-states
52. deer
53. women
54. geese
55. children
56. moose
57. mice
58. alumni
59. phenomena
60. cacti
61. analyses
62. criteria
63. the secretary's desk
64. the crowd's applause
65. Heather's birthday
66. the house's front door
67. Matt's ball glove
68. writers' dictionaries
69. doctors' calendars
70. ants' hills
71. countries' islands
72. geese's formations

▶ Pronouns

LESSON SUMMARY

Pronouns are more than "a word that takes the place of a noun." Learn about their categories and cases and the importance of making them agree in *number*, *gender*, and *person*.

ronouns take the place of, or refer to, a specific noun in a sentence. To use pronouns correctly, make sure that your pronoun agrees in gender, number, and person with the noun it is replacing or referring to (the antecedent, or referent noun).

▶ Gender

The English language has three genders: masculine, feminine, and neuter. The gender of a pronoun tells us whether it is replacing (or referring to) a masculine, feminine, or neuter noun. When referring to a male, *he, his,* and *him* is used; referring to a female, *she, her,* and *hers*; and to animals or things, *it* and *its*.

> **Examples:**
> Joseph took Wanda's car to the mechanic.
> **He** took her car to the mechanic.
> **He** took **it** to the mechanic.

In today's society, we are moving away from gender-specific titles and using more inclusive words, such as *police officer, fire fighter, mail carrier,* and *flight attendant, rather than policeman, fireman, mailman,* and *stewardess.* It is never correct, however, to refer to people as *it,* so the pronouns *he* and *she* must still be used when referring to a particular person.

▶ Number

A pronoun that takes the place of or refers to a singular noun (one person, place, or thing) must be singular as well. The same applies to plural pronouns and nouns.

> **Examples:**
> If an **employee** wants to park in the hospital parking lot, then **he or she** must apply for the appropriate tag to do so.
> **Employees** who need to renew **their** parking tags must show **their** current hospital ID cards.

Words like *anybody, anyone, everybody, everyone, each, neither, nobody,* and the like are singular and must take a singular pronoun:

> **Everybody** must have **his** or **her** ID card validated.

To avoid awkward language, it is sometimes better to recast the sentence in the plural:

> **Employees** must have **their** ID cards validated.

▶ Person

English grammar has three "persons": first, second, and third. First-person pronouns like *I, me, we,* and *us* include the speaker. Second-person pronouns involve only *you, your,* and *yours.* Third-person pronouns—*he, she, it, they, them,* and so on—include everybody else.

> **Examples:**
> **I** went with **my** family to Yellowstone State Park.
> **You** wouldn't have believed **your** eyes—the scenery was amazing.
> Doug said **he** would take photos with **his** new camera.

▶ Categories and Cases

Pronouns are divided into five categories: personal, demonstrative, relative, indefinite, and interrogative, and four cases: subjective, objective, possessive, and reflexive.

Personal Pronouns

Personal pronouns can refer to the speaker or speakers (first person), or to those being spoken to (second person), or to those who are spoken about (third person). The following table shows the subjective case personal pronouns, which are pronouns used as the subject of a sentence.

SUBJECTIVE CASE PERSONAL PRONOUNS			
	FIRST PERSON	**SECOND PERSON**	**THIRD PERSON**
Singular	I	you	he, she, it
Plural	we	you	they

In a sentence containing a pronoun, the word that the pronoun is referring to is called the antecedent.

Example:

Trent is a bricklayer. **He** builds homes and buildings.

The antecedent for the pronoun *he* is *Trent*.

Example:

Lydia took **her** to the bank.

Because there is no antecedent mentioned for the pronoun *her*, this sentence is unclear.

Objective case pronouns are pronouns that are used as objects (receivers of action) in a sentence. (See Lesson 11 for more information on objects.) The following table shows the objective case personal pronouns.

OBJECTIVE CASE PERSONAL PRONOUNS			
	FIRST PERSON	**SECOND PERSON**	**THIRD PERSON**
Singular	me	you	him, her, it
Plural	us	you	them

The following sentences show how objective case pronouns are used.

Please give **me** the envelope to put in the mailbox.
Should I send **him** to boarding school this year or not?
I gave **you** flowers for graduation, remember?

Personal pronouns can also show possession—whose something is. The following table shows the possessive case personal pronouns.

POSSESSIVE CASE PERSONAL PRONOUNS			
	FIRST PERSON	**SECOND PERSON**	**THIRD PERSON**
Singular	my, mine	your, yours	his, her, hers, its
Plural	our, ours	your, yours	their, theirs

The following sentences show how possessive case pronouns are used.

This old gray house is **mine**; the new white one over there is **his**.
Hers, around the corner, is getting **its** roof replaced. **My** roof probably needs replacing soon. **Our** neighbors are getting **their** driveway repaved.

Lastly, reflexive case pronouns, *selfish* pronouns, are used to show a subject performing some kind of action upon itself. Reflexive pronouns can only act as objects in a sentence, never as subjects. The following table shows the reflexive case personal pronouns.

REFLEXIVE CASE PERSONAL PRONOUNS			
	FIRST PERSON	**SECOND PERSON**	**THIRD PERSON**
Singular	myself	yourself	himself, herself, itself
Plural	ourselves	yourselves	themselves

The following sentences show how reflexive pronouns are used. Notice that they are only used as objects.

> He cut **himself** on the edge of the can while opening it.
> It was obvious they thought of **themselves** as experts.
> The computerized car drove **itself** during the demonstration.

Practice

Identify the case of the boldfaced pronouns in each of the sentences.

1. **It** turned out to be a beautiful day.

2. **I** asked Todd why the mail was sitting on the floor.

3. Only Lisa was able to finish **her** test on time.

4. **She** likes **their** fruit salad best.

5. **It** was supposed to rain again; the weather has been dreary lately.

6. Kenneth turned the corner recklessly in **his** new car and scratched **it**.

7. The squirrel balanced **itself** on the tree branch high above **me**.

8. Riley took **his** book and placed **it** on the table next to **him**.

9. **He** applied for a credit card online today and **they** approved **him**.

10. Liza had to buy **herself** a new pair of glasses because **her** sister accidentally sat on **them** and broke **them**.

Demonstrative Pronouns

The four **demonstrative pronouns**—*this, that, these,* and *those*—refer to things in relation to number and distance. These pronouns can act as a subject or an object, as the following table shows.

DEMONSTRATIVE PRONOUNS		
	SINGULAR	**PLURAL**
Near	this	these
Far	that	those

Demonstrative pronouns look like this in sentences.

> **This** tastes awful, Mom!
> I should take **these** and give them to Shelly.
> **Those** are his, not yours.
> I want **that** for my collection.

Relative Pronouns

The **relative pronouns**—*that, which, who,* and *whom*—relate (or refer back) to another noun that precedes it in the sentence, and introduce clauses that describe earlier nouns or pronouns.

> **Examples:**
> I own the boat **that** won the race.
> The man **who** drove it is my best friend, Jack.
> He is someone on **whom** I rely for skill and expertise.
> We have entered into the next race, **which** is on Friday.

Notice that *who* and *whom* refer to a person, while *which* and *that* refer to things. Use *that* to signify information that is necessary (restrictive) to the meaning of the sentence, and *which* to signify information that is discretionary (nonrestrictive), in that even if it is removed, the meaning of the sentence is not altered.

Indefinite Pronouns

Indefinite pronouns refer to unspecified people, places, or things. Some indefinite pronouns are always singular, some are always plural, and others can be both, depending on what or whom they're referring to. See the following table for the classifications.

INDEFINITE PRONOUNS				
SINGULAR			**PLURAL**	**BOTH**
another	anyone	no one	both	all
anybody	anything	nobody	few	most
everyone	everybody	one	many	none
everything	nothing	someone	several	some
each	either	somebody		
something				

Here are some examples of how indefinite pronouns are used in sentences.

> **Both** of his in-laws took their nieces camping in Jackson Hole, Wyoming.
> **Each** girl brought her journal with her.
> **All** of the campers are expected to keep their site litter-free.

Interrogative Pronouns

Interrogative pronouns are pronouns that begin questions: *who, whom, whose, which,* and *what.*

> **Examples:**
> **Who** put the milk in the freezer?
> **What** is the sum of 12 and 31?
> To **whom** does this black jacket belong?
> **Which** direction do I head to get to Spring Lake?
> **Whose** pen is on the floor over there?

When these pronouns are not acting as interrogative pronouns, they also play the roles of relative and personal pronouns in sentences.

Practice

Determine whether the boldfaced pronoun is *demonstrative, relative, indefinite,* or *interrogative.*

11. **No one** is supposed to be going.

12. **That** is the best idea I've heard all day.

13. The supervisor gave her the Monroe account **that** needed immediate attention.

14. **Whose** idea was it to paint the deck red?

15. Chris told me that **somebody** saw **someone** on your bike.

16. It was Greg **who** called our house at two o'clock this morning.

17. If **no one** helps **anybody**, then what is the point of continuing?

18. **What** can I say? I planned **this** from the get-go.

19. Ever since last year, **few** have stayed on, except for Charlie.

20. They played the team **that** had a horrible losing streak, and lost.

▶ Answers

1. **It**: subjective
2. **I**: subjective
3. **her**: possessive
4. **She**: subjective; **their**: objective
5. **It**: subjective
6. **his**: possessive; **it**: objective
7. **itself**: reflexive; **me**: objective
8. **his**: possessive; **it**: objective; **him**: objective
9. **He**: subjective; **they**: subjective; **him**: objective
10. **herself**: reflexive; **her**: possessive; **them, them**: objective

11. **No one**: indefinite
12. **That**: demonstrative
13. **that**: relative
14. **Whose**: interrogative
15. **somebody**: indefinite; **someone**: indefinite
16. **who**: relative
17. **no one**: indefinite; **anybody**: indefinite
18. **What**: interrogative; **this**: demonstrative
19. **few**: indefinite
20. **that**: relative

Verbs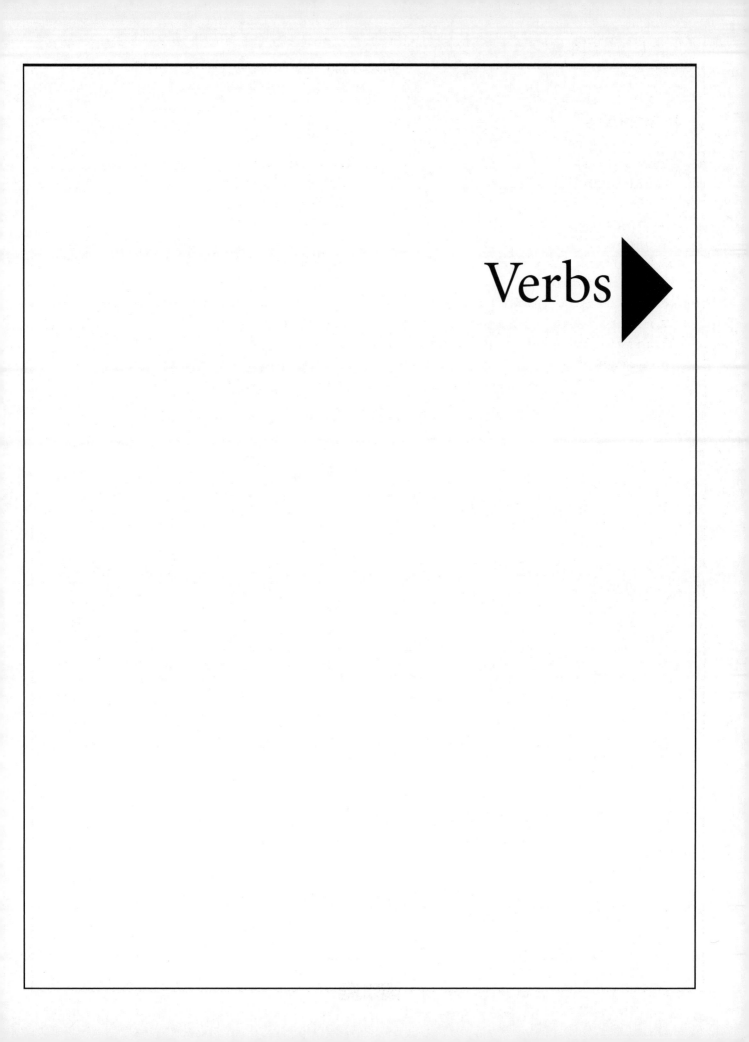

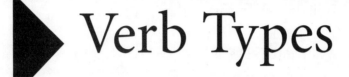# Verb Types

LESSON SUMMARY

Some action and linking verbs look the same. Learn how to tell the difference, and get some help with helping verbs along the way.

This chapter covers three types of verbs: action verbs, linking verbs, and helping verbs.

▶ Action Verbs

Most **action verbs** represent a visible action, one that can be seen with our eyes. For example, *waltz*, *surf*, *gallop*, *chop*, *row*, *swing*, and *punch* are action verbs.

Identifying such *doing words* in a sentence is generally easy. But some action verbs are more difficult to identify because the action is far less obvious, as in *depend*, *yearn*, *foresee*, *understand*, *consider*, *require*, *mean*, *remember*, and *suppose*. It is helpful to remember that *mental* verbs are action verbs too, even though they are less visible than the others.

Practice

Identify the action verbs in the following sentences.

1. I assumed that you would bring your swimsuit because the invitation stated "pool party."

2. Placing your name on the list increases your chances of being selected for the part.

3. Many people have the ill-conceived notion that "natural" means pesticide-free.

4. The supermarket will open again tomorrow at 9:00 A.M.

5. Having a picnic at the park can be a fun way to spend time with your family.

6. Alex's laptop wouldn't reboot after the unexpected power surge at the office earlier in the day.

7. Brush corn on the cob with butter and salt, wrap it in heavy-duty aluminum foil, and roast it on the grill for a delicious treat.

▶ Linking Verbs

Unlike the action verb, the **linking verb** expresses a state of being or a condition. Specifically, it links, or connects, a noun with an adjective (a descriptor) or another noun (an identifier) in a sentence.

Example:
Nathan and Sara **are** hardworking students.

The noun **students** identifies or renames the compound subjects, *Nathan and Sara*; *hardworking* is an adjective describing the noun *students*; and the verb *are* links the two components together.

Example:
Collin **was** tired after his golf game.

The adjective *tired* describes the subject, Collin, and the verb *was* links the two components together.

Some linking verbs can be tricky to identify because they appear to be action verbs. Their job in the sentence is to clarify the condition or state of the noun to which they are connected. The verbs in the following list can act not only as action verbs, but also as linking verbs.

appear	become	feel	grow	look
prove	remain	seem	smell	sound
stay	taste	come	lie	prove
act	turn	fall	get	

How can one tell what role these tricky verbs are playing? Let's take a look at the word *turned*, used in two different ways.

The Ferris wheel **turned** slowly as it began its initial rotation.

Here, the Ferris wheel performed an action: it *turned*. Can you visualize the huge wheel slowly rotating, with the riders in the cars, as it warms up? The word *turned* here is an action-oriented verb. Let's look at another example:

One frightened rider **turned** green as the ride began to speed up quickly.

Here, the word *turned* connects the describing word, or adjective—*green*—to the subject—*rider*. In this example, *turned* is acting as a linking verb, not an action verb.

LINKING VERBS							
am	is	are	was	were	be	being	been

One easy way to tell whether a verb is an action verb or a linking verb is to replace the verb in question with a verb form of *be* (from the preceding table), or a linking verb like *seemed* or *became*. If the new sentence still makes sense, then you have a linking verb. If the sentence loses its meaning, then you have an action verb. For instance:

> The farmer **grew** several prize-winning tomatoes this season.

Let's replace *grew* with *is*:

> The farmer **is** several prize-winning tomatoes this season.

Or, let's use the word *seemed*:

> The farmer **seemed** several prize-winning tomatoes this season.

Neither choice works, which means that *grew* is an action verb, not a linking verb, in this sentence.

Let's try another example.

> The beef stew we had for dinner **tasted** delicious.

This time, let's replace *tasted* with *was*:

> The beef stew we had for dinner **was** delicious.

Or, let's use the word *looked*:

> The beef stew we had for dinner **looked** delicious.

Both choices make sense, because in this sentence *tasted* is a linking verb, not an action verb.

Practice

Determine whether the boldfaced verbs in the following sentences are action or linking verbs.

8. "It **appears** that the only solution to this problem is starting over," said Trudy.

9. "The group **appears** dismayed at that prospect," she thought to herself.

10. Dennis was asked to **prove** beyond a shadow of a doubt that the butler did it.

11. There was no doubt in his adversary's mind that his argument would **prove** faulty.

12. The sign says to **stay** behind the line when viewing the work of art.

13. We **stayed** quiet while the tour guide explained the painting.

14. We **tasted** the orange sherbet and ordered a pint to take home.

15. We decided that it **tasted** delicious.

▶ Helping Verbs

Helping verbs enhance the main verb's meaning by providing us with more information about its tense.

COMMON HELPING VERBS								
am	is	are	was	were	be	do	does	did
have	had	has	may	might	must	shall	will	can
should	would	could	ought					

A main verb may have as many as three helping verbs in front of it in a sentence.

Examples:
Martin **walked** quickly to the bus stop to avoid being late.
Martin **had walked** quickly to the bus stop to avoid being late.
Martin **must have walked** quickly to the bus stop to avoid being late.

A main verb with helping verbs is called a **verb phrase**. It is important to remember that a helping verb need not be right next to the main verb in the sentence. For instance, we could rewrite the last sentence in such a way that the adverb *quickly* separates the helping verbs *must* and *have* from the main verb *walked*.

Example:
Martin **must have** quickly **walked** to the bus stop to avoid being late.

If you were asked to identify the verb phrase, you would eliminate the adverb *quickly* and give *must have walked* as the answer.

Note that adverbs are typically (but not always) words ending in *-ly*. Some other adverbs are *very*, *so*, *more*, and *not*.

Practice
Identify the verb phrases in the following sentences.

16. We could have driven to the city, but we took the train instead.

17. Nancy would not have thrown the paper away if she had known it was important.

18. William had already read the book twice, so he must have easily discussed it with the teacher.

19. Next time, if you should need help, please feel free to ask. I would be very happy to help.

20. The dealer will go to the flea market to find good antique deals.

21. I didn't realize that she had already gone; otherwise, I would have given her the money earlier.

22. The skier might have won the race had she not gotten her pole stuck in the snow.

► Answers

1. assumed, bring, stated
2. increases, selected
3. means
4. open
5. spend
6. reboot
7. Brush, wrap, roast
8. action
9. linking
10. action
11. linking
12. action
13. linking
14. action
15. linking
16. could have driven
17. would have thrown, had known
18. had read, must have discussed
19. should need, would be
20. will go
21. did realize, had gone, would have given
22. might have won, had gotten

▶ Regular and Irregular Verbs

LESSON SUMMARY

Become better acquainted with the pesky past-tense verbs that DON'T end with *-ed*, and learn about proper usage with tricky verbs such as *lay/lie* and *sit/set*.

ost, but not all, verbs follow a simple and predictable pattern when expressing past action: They end in *-ed*. These types of verbs, called **regular verbs**, can be changed from the present tense to the past tense by simply adding *-ed* or *-d*.

Example:

    Those musicians **play** jazz music well. Last evening, though, they surprised the crowd and **played** some blues pieces.

Irregular verbs, on the other hand, do not follow any type of pattern when forming the past tense and require memorization.

Example:

    "**Put** the tennis racquets away in the storage bin, please," said Coach. "I **put** them away already," replied Kevin.

Here, the irregular verb *put* stays the same whether it is past or present. Other verbs that follow suit are *cost*, *burst*, *bid*, *cut*, and *set*, to name a few.

Here is a list of common irregular verbs.

COMMON IRREGULAR VERBS

PRESENT	PAST	PAST PARTICIPLE
be	was/were	been
beat	beat	beaten
become	became	become
begin	began	begun
bite	bit	bitten
blow	blew	blown
break	broke	broken
bring	brought	brought
broadcast	broadcast	broadcast
build	built	built
buy	bought	bought
catch	caught	caught
choose	chose	chosen
come	came	come
cost	cost	cost
cut	cut	cut
do	did	done
draw	drew	drawn
drink	drank	drunk
drive	drove	driven
eat	ate	eaten
fall	fell	fallen
feed	fed	fed
feel	felt	felt
fight	fought	fought
find	found	found
fly	flew	flown

COMMON IRREGULAR VERBS *(Continued)*

PRESENT	PAST	PAST PARTICIPLE
forbid	forbade	forbidden
forget	forgot	forgotten
forgive	forgave	forgiven
freeze	froze	frozen
get	got	gotten
give	gave	given
go	went	gone
grow	grew	grown
hang	hung	hung
have	had	had
hear	heard	heard
hide	hid	hidden
hit	hit	hit
hold	held	held
hurt	hurt	hurt
keep	kept	kept
know	knew	known
lay	laid	laid
lead	led	led
learn	learned/learnt	learned/learnt
leave	left	left
lend	lent	lent
let	let	let
lie	lay	lain
light	lit	lit
lose	lost	lost
make	made	made

(Continued)

COMMON IRREGULAR VERBS (Continued)

PRESENT	PAST	PAST PARTICIPLE
mean	meant	meant
meet	met	met
mistake	mistook	mistaken
mow	mowed	mowed/mown
pay	paid	paid
proofread	proofread	proofread
put	put	put
quit	quit	quit
read	read	read
ride	rode	ridden
ring	rang	rung
rise	rose	risen
run	ran	run
say	said	said
see	saw	seen
seek	sought	sought
sell	sold	sold
send	sent	sent
sew	sewed	sewed/sewn
shake	shook	shaken
shave	shaved	shaved/shaven
shine	shone	shone
shoot	shot	shot
show	showed	showed/shown
shrink	shrank	shrunk
shut	shut	shut

COMMON IRREGULAR VERBS (Continued)

PRESENT	PAST	PAST PARTICIPLE
sing	sang	sung
sink	sank	sunk
sit	sat	sat
sleep	slept	slept
slide	slid	slid/slidden
speak	spoke	spoken
speed	speeded/sped	speeded/sped
spend	spent	spent
spread	spread	spread
spring	sprang	sprung
stand	stood	stood
steal	stole	stolen
stick	stuck	stuck
sting	stung	stung
strike	struck	struck/stricken
strive	strove	striven/strived
swear	swore	sworn
swim	swam	swum
take	took	taken
teach	taught	taught
tear	tore	torn
tell	told	told
think	thought	thought
throw	threw	thrown
understand	understood	understood
upset	upset	upset

(Continued)

COMMON IRREGULAR VERBS *(Continued)*		
PRESENT	**PAST**	**PAST PARTICIPLE**
wake	woke	woken
wear	wore	worn
weep	wept	wept
win	won	won
wind	wound	wound
write	wrote	written

Practice

Determine whether the boldfaced verb in the sentence is correct. Make any necessary corrections.

1. Tomorrow, we **will left** early in the morning for the airport.

2. Mr. Brown, our neighbor, **spend** the weekend cleaning his pool.

3. The sun **shine** brightly all day today.

4. I was beginning to **has** second thoughts about quitting.

5. We are **watched** the game from the privacy of the box.

6. For now, we **will head** north, then east.

7. Mom **sewn** me a new set of placemats for the picnic table each summer.

8. When I was little, I was often **mistook** for my twin sister by acquaintances.

9. Yesterday, our band **practiced** at Joe's house.

10. I need help **cut** the vegetables for tonight's dinner.

► Problem Verbs

Conjugating irregular verbs can be a bit challenging in itself. But there are two pairs of irregular verbs that present an additional challenge because they sound alike even though they do not mean the same thing: *lay/lie* and *set/sit*.

LAY OR LIE			
PRESENT	**PRESENT PARTICIPLE**	**PAST**	**PAST PARTICIPLE**
lay, lays	(am, is, are, was) **laying**	**laid**	(have, has) **laid**

To *lay* means to *place or put* an object somewhere. This object, a noun, must always follow the verb *lay*, making that noun what we call a direct object—the object that directly receives the action from the verb it follows.

Example:

Martin **laid** the blanket on the grass before **laying** the basket of delicious food on it.

PRESENT	**PRESENT PARTICIPLE**	**PAST**	**PAST PARTICIPLE**
lie, lies	(am, is, are, was) **lying**	**lay**	(have, has) **lain**

To *lie* means to *rest or recline* or to *be situated*. Instead of a noun, a prepositional phrase or an adverb usually follows the verb to complete the sentence or thought.

Example:

The large old oak tree **lies** at the edge of the field. The cattle **have lain** in its shade for over a century.

In these sentences, the prepositional phrases *at the edge, of the field, in its shade*, and *for over a century* clarify the writer's thought. Phrases such as these are very useful for adding vivid details to writing. (See Lesson 10 for more information.) Without them, we would just have the two rather boring phrases *the large old oak tree lies* and *the cattle have lain*.

Practice

In each sentence, select the correct form of the verb *lay* or *lie*.

11. Sylvia has (laid, lain) on the sofa all afternoon in despair.

12. The broken bottle (lay, laid) at the side of the road unnoticed.

13. Jason should find his camera (laying, lying) in the back of his closet.

14. The old dog has (lain, laid) on the front porch every day for years.

15. Bianca (lay, laid) her scissors on the counter and picked up the brush.

16. The new bride and her groom (lie, lay) their wedding photos on the table.

17. Grandma complained she had (laid, lain) awake for hours before falling asleep last night.

18. Thom (laid, lain) the racquet on the bench and went to get a cool drink of water.

19. Dad says he is (laying, lying) new carpet in the den next Wednesday.

20. The map shows that the treasure chest is (laying, lying) just below this rock.

SET OR SIT			
PRESENT	**PRESENT PARTICIPLE**	**PAST**	**PAST PARTICIPLE**
set, sets	(am, is, are, was) **setting**	**set**	(have, has) **set**

To *set* means to *place or put* an object someplace. Like the verb *lay*, it must be followed by a noun.

Example:

A harried young mother **sets** her groceries on the counter and tends to her crying son. She **has set** a pillow on the sofa for his nap.

PRESENT	**PRESENT PARTICIPLE**	**PAST**	**PAST PARTICIPLE**
sit, sits	(am, is, are, was) **sitting**	**sat**	(have, has) **sat**

To *sit* means to *be situated* or to *be seated or resting*. Like the verb *lie*, it is usually followed by a prepositional phrase or an adverb for further clarification.

Example:

I usually **sit** in the front row of the theater for an unobstructed view of the performance. When I **have sat** further back, I found I could not see the actors well.

Practice

In each sentence, select the correct form of the verb *set* or *sit*.

21. The audience (set, sat) patiently as the stage crew changed the scene.

22. My favorite photograph of my cat Milo (sits, sets) on my dresser.

23. (Setting, Sitting) good examples for younger children is important.

24. I was told to (set, sit) my empty glass in the sink.

25. Four students (set, sat) their reports on my desk before the due date.

26. Hotel rooms often have a rack to (set, sit) your luggage on.

27. There are many trophies (setting, sitting) in the case by the front lobby.

28. The owner (set, sat) the pool umbrellas around the facility before opening.

29. Jane and Robert are (setting, sitting) together at the table chatting.

30. The winding river (sets, sits) just at the foot of the hills.

▶ Other Tricky Verbs

Several other verbs need special attention in order to be used correctly.

Most likely, the reason why *accept* and *except* are often misused is because they sound alike. Their meanings, however, are very different. To *accept* means to approve, agree, or willingly receive, whereas *except* is really a preposition that means excluding or unless.

Example:

I would **accept** your apology for being late today, but **except** for yesterday, you have been late every day this week.

If you're still confused about whether to *except* or *accept*, remember that when you are agreeing with, or *accepting*, something, you are "**CC**-eeing" eye to eye with someone; but when you make an *exception*, you are "**X**-cluding" something in that agreement.

Another pair of verbs often confused in ordinary speech is *can* and *may*.

Can means having the ability to do something. When you say *Can I help you?* what you're really asking is whether you *have the ability* to help this person. (Unless you're completely indisposed in some way, the question leads one to wonder why you would ask it in the first place!)

May, on the other hand, means having permission to do something. When you say *May I help you?* you are asking someone to *allow* you to help him or her.

Example:

I **can** help you rake leaves this afternoon only after I finish my other chores. **May** I help you with it tomorrow instead?

The verbs *hang* and *lie* are unusual in that they can be either regular or irregular, depending on their meaning in the sentence. If *hang* refers to a thief going to the gallows to hang, then it is a regular verb, and should be conjugated *hang, hanged, hanged*. But if it is used in the sense of *hanging out with friends* or *hanging a picture on the wall*, for instance, then it is an irregular verb, and should be conjugated *hang, hung, hung*. Similarly, when *lie* means telling an untruth, it is a regular verb and should be conjugated *lie, lied, lied*. When it means to recline, it is an irregular verb, which we learned to conjugate earlier in this lesson.

Practice

In each sentence, select the correct verb to complete the sentence.

31. Nathan carefully (hanged, hung) the mirror on the wall behind his dresser.

32. (Except, Accept) for the annoying mosquitoes, we had a great camping trip.

33. I cannot (accept, except) this answer without an explanation.

34. You (can, may) have a third helping of mashed potatoes if you like.

35. Without hesitation, the king sentenced the criminal to be (hung, hanged).

36. (Can, May) the clown walk the tightrope without the umbrella?

▶ Answers

1. incorrect, **will leave**
2. incorrect, **spent**
3. incorrect, **shone**
4. incorrect, **have**
5. incorrect, **watching**
6. correct
7. incorrect, **sewed**
8. incorrect, **mistaken**
9. correct
10. incorrect, **cutting**
11. lain
12. lay
13. lying
14. lain
15. laid
16. lay
17. lain
18. laid
19. laying
20. lying
21. sat
22. sits
23. Setting
24. set
25. set
26. set
27. sitting
28. set
29. sitting
30. sits
31. hung
32. Except
33. accept
34. may
35. hanged
36. Can

L E S S O N

6 ▶ Verb Forms and Tenses

LESSON SUMMARY

Having a basic understanding of the *four verb forms* is essential to forming verb tenses properly. In addition, learn how to form tenses from *basic* to *perfects* through the *progressives*.

Verb tenses are very useful in our spoken and written language because they help our listeners and readers understand *when* it is that something we are referring to is happening. The tricky thing about tenses is that we need to be consistent with them so as to minimize confusion. In order to form verb tenses properly, we must have a basic understanding of the four different verb forms of the English language.

▶ Verb Forms

Verb forms may look similar to tenses, but they are not. Learning the following basic forms, or principal parts, will help you when forming verb tenses later in this lesson.

Present

The **present** form of a verb is usually the first entry you find when you consult a dictionary (e.g., *care, forgive, think,* etc.). Sometimes an *-s* is added to the end of the present form of the verb when it is used in conjunction with a singular noun. For instance, *she cares, he forgives, it means.*

Present Participle

The **present participle** is made by adding the suffix *-ing* to the present form; it is always accompanied by a *be* verb (see Lesson 5 for a full list), which acts as a helping verb, forming what is called a **verb phrase**, such as *am caring, is forgiving, were thinking,* and so forth. Notice that this verb form expresses action that is ongoing.

Past

The **past** form of a verb shows actions that happened in the past (e.g., *cared, forgave, thought*). Remember that all regular verbs in the past tense end in *-ed,* whereas irregular verbs end in a variety of ways.

Past Participle

The **past participle** of a verb consists of its past form, accompanied by the helping verb *have, has,* or *had* (e.g., *have cared, has forgiven, had thought,* etc.). This is true of both regular and irregular verbs.

SOME REGULAR VERB FORMS			
PRESENT	**PRESENT PARTICIPLE***	**PAST**	**PAST PARTICIPLE****
care, cares	am caring	cared	have cared
yell, yells	are yelling	yelled	have yelled

SOME IRREGULAR VERB FORMS			
PRESENT	**PRESENT PARTICIPLE***	**PAST**	**PAST PARTICIPLE****
think, thinks	was thinking	thought	have thought
grow, grows	were growing	grew	has grown

IRREGULAR VERBS WHOSE FORM DOES NOT CHANGE			
PRESENT	**PRESENT PARTICIPLE***	**PAST**	**PAST PARTICIPLE****
cost, costs	is costing	cost	has cost
put, puts	am putting	put	have put

*uses *am, is, are, was,* or *were* as helping verb

**uses *have, has,* or *had* as helping verb

▶ Verb Tenses

All verb tenses are formed by utilizing one of the four principal parts of the verb. When we combine these parts with different pronouns, we can see all the different forms that a verb can take in a given tense; this is called **verb conjugation**.

CONJUGATING THE IRREGULAR VERBS *BRING* AND *DO*		
	SINGULAR	**PLURAL**
PRESENT TENSE		
First person	I bring, do	we bring, do
Second person	you bring, do	you bring, do
Third person	he, she, it brings, does	they bring, do
PAST TENSE		
First person	I brought, did	we brought, did
Second person	you brought, did	you brought, did
Third person	he, she, it brought, did	they brought, did
FUTURE TENSE		
First person	I will bring, will do	we will bring, will do
Second person	you will bring, will do	you will bring, will do
Third person	he, she, it will bring, will do	they will bring, will do

We are most familiar with three basic tenses:

Present. The present tense shows present action or action that happens on a regular basis.

Example:
He **writes** articles for a local newspaper.

Past. The past tense indicates that the action has already happened.

Example:
He **wrote** several award-winning articles.

Future. The future tense tells us that the action has not yet happened, but will.

Example:
He **will write** an editorial for *Time* this month.

Practice

Choose the correct verb and identify the tense in the following sentences.

1. Jack will (paint, paints, painted) houses in the summer for extra spending money.

2. Yesterday, Anaya's car (break, broke, broken) down on the turnpike.

3. It is advisable that you (carry, carries, carried) your insurance card with you at all times.

4. (Put, Puts) the remainder of the supplies in the storage room down the hall.

5. The load of dirt (cost, costs) him more than anticipated.

In addition to the three basic verb tenses—present, past, and future—we have a number of tenses that more precisely pinpoint the timing or progress of the actions that we speak of.

Present Progressive. The present progressive tense shows action that is currently in progress. The present progressive is formed by combining the present tense of the verb *be* with the present participle of the verb.

> **Example:**
> Robert and Olivia **are running** the charity auction at the church.

Past Progressive. The past progressive tense indicates that the action happened at some specific time in the past. The past progressive is formed by combining the past tense of the verb *be* with the present participle of the verb.

> **Example:**
> Jennifer **was watching** the lottery drawing on TV last night.

Future Progressive. The future progressive tense tells us that the action is continuous or will occur in the future. The future progressive is formed by combining the future tense of the verb *be* with the present participle of the verb.

> **Example:**
> Wanda **will be traveling** to Provence next winter.

Practice

Choose the correct verb and identify the tense in the following sentences.

6. It is likely that the child was (run, runs, running) when she slipped and fell.

7. I will be (seeing, saw, seen) the play *Les Miserables* on Broadway in New York City.

8. Sometimes an old model (stay, stayed, stays) more popular than a new one.

9. It seems that the phone (rings, rang, rung) when I was away from my desk.

10. Joseph is (get, got, getting) another opinion from a nearby vet.

Present Perfect. The present perfect tense shows that the action was started in the past and continues up to the present time. The present perfect is formed by combining *have* or *has* with the past participle of the verb.

> **Example:**
> People **have used** money as a means of exchange since about 1200 B.C.

Past Perfect. The past perfect tense indicates that the action happened in the past and was completed before some other past action was begun. The past perfect is formed by combining the helping verb *had* with the past participle of the verb.

Example:
> Before that, many **had bartered** for the goods they wanted with shells, livestock, and agriculture.

Future Perfect. The future perfect tense tells us that the action will start and finish in the future. The future perfect is formed by combining the helping verbs *will have*, *would have*, or *will have been* with the past participle of the verb.

Example:
> As of 2010, the U.S. dollar will have been used by its citizens as national currency for about 225 years.

Practice

Choose the correct verb and identify the tense in the following sentences.

11. The audience was (laugh, laughing, laughed) at the clown in the ring.

12. We will have (cover, covers, covered) 3,000 miles on our trip by the time we return home next week.

13. Last week, her doctor (recommended, recommends) that she stay off of her injured ankle for several days.

14. Cheryl had (pay, paid, pays) the bill on time.

15. The editor would have (reply, replies, replied) to most of the comments by now, but couldn't because he was occupied with other issues.

16. Jeff was (hold, held, holding) the flowers behind his back when he approached his wife.

17. The club (enjoy, enjoys, enjoying) the camping trip in Washington each year.

18. His story (become, becoming, became) more convoluted each time he told it.

19. Alice had (write, writes, written) many letters before she received a reply.

20. Carla, the librarian, has (preview, previews, previewed) many children's books before placing them on the shelves.

A ghastly grammatical error that should be avoided is interchanging the words *of* and *have* in writing. Consider the term *should've*, as in "I *should've* gone with the blue, not the green." It's a common misconception that the term *should of*, not "should have," is being said, and it is then duly written as such. Be careful! The terms *could've* and *would've* (translated into *could of* and *would of*) fall in this trap as well.

► **Answers**

1. **will paint:** future tense
2. **broke:** past tense
3. **carry:** present tense
4. **Put:** present tense
5. **cost:** past tense
6. **was running:** past progressive tense
7. **will be seeing:** future progressive tense
8. **stays:** present tense
9. **rang:** past tense
10. **is getting:** present progressive tense

11. **was laughing:** past progressive tense
12. **will have covered:** future perfect tense
13. **recommended:** past tense
14. **had paid:** past perfect tense
15. **would have replied:** past perfect tense
16. **was holding:** past progressive tense
17. **enjoys:** present tense
18. **became:** past tense
19. **had written:** past perfect tense
20. **has previewed:** present perfect tense

Modifiers

LESSON

7 ▶ Adjectives

LESSON SUMMARY

There's more to this modifier than describing. Learn to identify articles, demonstratives, possessives, and comparatives as well.

djectives are used to give the listener or reader more specific information about a noun or pronoun. For instance, if a group of people were asked to think of the word *car*, each one would have a different visual image. That's because the word *car* by iself is too general. But if the words *red* and *Corvette* were added, the visual images would be more similar because the car has been more specifically described. An adjective is what we call a **modifier**; it answers any of three specific questions about the noun(s) or pronoun(s) it is modifying: *what kind?* (*friendly, robust, spiky*), *which one(s)?* (*this, that, these, those*), and *how many?* (*nine, few, many, some*).

While adjectives typically come before the noun(s) they are modifying, they may come afterward, too.

Example:

The roller coaster, **large** and **intimidating**, loomed high above all other rides at the park, tantalizing the most daring of park visitors.

57

Practice

Identify the common adjectives in the following sentences.

1. Carl used his new cell phone to call his younger brother, Mike.

2. The library is a good place to study because it is quiet.

3. Mrs. Franklin was enthusiastic about going to the gym.

4. My fishing pole was shorter than his.

5. The blue cheese dressing had a sharp, but appealing, taste.

6. I found the perfect birthday card for my niece at the store.

7. The soft white sand at the beach was warm.

▶ Articles

Three words that we use in our everyday language—*a*, *an*, and *the*—are special adjectives that we call **articles**. There are two types of articles: the definite article (*the*), which implies something specific (not just any roadmap but this particular roadmap) and the indefinite article (*a* or *an*), which is nonspecific (pick a roadmap; any one will do).

Sometimes deciding whether to use *a* or *an* can be tricky. The best way to decide is to follow your ears. The word *igloo*, for instance, begins with an initial vowel sound (short *i*), so it takes the indefinite article *an*. The word *ferocious*, on the other hand, begins with an initial consonant sound (*f*), so it takes the indefinite article *a*. Don't let the beginning letter fool you. For instance, the word *one* begins with a vowel, but has an initial consonant sound (*w*), which means it takes *a*, not *an*.

Practice

Correctly place the indefinite article *a* or *an* in front of each word.

8. hour

9. octagon

10. university

11. knife

12. banjo

13. upperclassman

14. honorable man

15. hallway

16. unopened box

17. excellent bargain

18. youth

19. one-way street

20. universal truth

21. quarter-century

22. hose reel

▶ Proper Adjectives

Proper adjectives look like proper nouns because they're capitalized, but they are modifying a noun, and therefore are adjectives. The phrases *English tea*, *Wilson family*, and *Chinese yo-yo* begin with a proper adjective, each answering the question *what kind?* or *which one?* about the noun it is modifying:

What kind of tea?	English
Which family?	Wilson
What kind of yo-yo?	Chinese

Practice

Determine whether the boldfaced word is a proper noun or a proper adjective in the following sentences.

23. The **Italian** flag is red, white, and green.

24. Her father visits **Italy** often.

25. While in **France**, we visited the Louvre.

26. The **French** Louvre is a world-famous art museum.

27. The **Hollywood** director had unparalleled talent.

28. **Hollywood** is part of the city of Los Angeles.

▶ Pronouns as Adjectives

A **pronoun** such as *he*, *she*, or *it* takes the place of another noun. If a noun can play the role of an adjective, so, too, can a pronoun. Some personal pronouns fall into the category of possessive adjectives: *my, your, his, her, its, our, their*. Take care not to confuse possessive adjectives with the possessive pronouns *mine, yours, his, hers, ours, theirs*. (You can review pronouns in Lesson 3.) While possessive pronouns can stand alone, a noun must follow possessive adjectives, which answer *which one?* about the noun that follows.

Examples:
Ronald took **his** *lawnmower* to the repair shop.
Victoria and Charles balanced **their** *checkbook* together.
Sara cleaned **her** *room* until it sparkled.

For comparison, here are a few sentences using possessive pronouns. Notice that here the object does *not* follow the pronoun.

That *lawnmower* is **his**.
Those *checkbooks* are **theirs**.
The clean *room* is **hers**.

Practice

Determine whether the boldfaced word is a possessive adjective or a possessive pronoun in the following sentences.

29. **His** flying lesson was scheduled for Friday, July 6.

30. Kyle was relieved that the weekend would be **his** to do what he wanted.

31. **My** unusual way of playing the guitar fascinated **my** instructor.

32. **Her** memo said that the account would remain **theirs** until further notice.

33. **Ours** floated effortlessly down the stream, a good 50 yards from **his**.

34. Get **your** feet wet first and it'll be downhill from there.

35. This one is **mine**, that one's **yours**.

36. How do you know **its** wing is injured?

▶ Demonstrative Adjectives

Like possessive adjectives, **demonstrative adjectives** (*this, that, these, those*) answer *which one?* about the object, but they always appear *before* the noun being modified.

> Examples:
>
> **That** <u>pool</u> looks so inviting on **this** sweltering day.
>
> **This** <u>channel</u> always seems to have so many commercials.
>
> **These** <u>flowers</u> are exceptionally beautiful in **that** vase.
>
> **Those** <u>shoes</u> are so much more comfortable than **that** pair.

If the word *this, that, these, or those* is not followed by a noun, but is *replacing* a noun in the sentence, it is considered a pronoun.

> Examples:
>
> **This** is broken.
>
> **That** belongs to Shera.
>
> **These** are sharp. Be careful.
>
> **Those** smell rotten.

Practice

Determine whether the boldfaced word is a demonstrative adjective or a demonstrative pronoun in the following sentences.

37. **This** is really over the top!

38. I haven't had **this** kind of chili before. It's delicious.

39. Please don't touch **these**, as they are very fragile.

40. **These** figures seem a bit high, but I'll concede.

41. **That** didn't make any sense to me; did it to you?

42. I'll have **that** one on the right, please.

43. What's **that**? I've never seen **that** species before.

44. **That** umbrella is sturdier than **this** one. We should take a couple of **those** instead.

▶ Comparative Adjectives

In the course of writing and speaking, it is often necessary to show how one thing compares to another. We can do this on three different levels with adjectives: the positive degree, the comparative degree, and the superlative degree.

In the positive degree, a simple statement is made about the noun:

> This sushi is **good**.

In the comparative degree, a comparison is made between two nouns:

> This sushi is good, but that one is **better**.

In the superlative degree, a comparison is made among more than two nouns:

Of all the sushi, this is the **best**.

Here are some rules to remember in forming the comparative or the superlative degree:

Rule 1. Add *-er* and *-est* to most one-syllable adjectives, like *small, smaller, smallest; hot, hotter, hottest.* Some one-syllable adjectives are irregular, like *good* (*good, better, best*), *bad* (*bad, worse, worst*), and *many* (*many, more, most*).

Rule 2. For adjectives of two or more syllables, use *more* and *most* to enhance the degree, or *less* and *least* to decrease the degree.

Examples:
> *agreeable*: *more* agreeable, *most* agreeable; *less* agreeable, *least* agreeable
> *spotted*: *more* spotted, *most* spotted; *less* spotted, *least* spotted

Of course, there are always exceptions. Here are some two-syllable adjectives that allow you to use *-er* and *-iest* in the comparative degree. Note that the final *y* is changed to an *i* before the endings are added.

> *happy, happier, happiest*
> *picky, pickier, pickiest*
> *silly, sillier, silliest*

Lastly, some adjectives just cannot be compared no matter how hard you try; they are called absolute adjectives or incomparables. Consider, for instance, the word *round.* How could something be *rounder* than *round*? Or take the word *unique*: How can something that is already one-of-a-kind be *more unique*? Other absolute adjectives are *favorite, true, false, perfect, square, free,* and *complete.*

Practice
Determine which form of the adjective best completes each of the following sentences.

45. Her (most high, highest) score at bowling was 200.

46. It goes without saying that Roger's hand was (larger, more large) than mine.

47. Jessica was (more good, better) than Jason at solving riddles.

48. This test tube of water is definitely (clearer, clearest) than the other.

49. Tomorrow's weather should be (coolest, cooler) than today's.

50. Compared to Darleen's cats, mine is hardly the (slimmest, slimmer).

51. Mike is (preciser, more precise) than Harrison with measurements.

► Answers

1. new, younger
2. good, quiet
3. enthusiastic
4. shorter
5. blue cheese, sharp, appealing
6. perfect, birthday
7. soft, white, warm
8. an
9. an
10. a
11. a
12. a
13. an
14. an
15. a
16. an
17. an
18. a
19. a
20. a
21. a
22. a
23. proper adjective
24. proper noun
25. proper noun
26. proper adjective

27. proper adjective
28. proper noun
29. possessive adjective
30. possessive pronoun
31. possessive adjective, possessive adjective
32. possessive adjective, possessive pronoun
33. possessive pronoun, possessive pronoun
34. possessive adjective
35. possessive pronoun, possessive pronoun
36. possessive adjective
37. demonstrative pronoun
38. demonstrative adjective
39. demonstrative pronoun
40. demonstrative adjective
41. demonstrative pronoun
42. demonstrative adjective
43. demonstrative pronoun, demonstrative adjective
44. demonstrative adjective, demonstrative adjective, demonstrative pronoun
45. highest
46. larger
47. better
48. clearer
49. cooler
50. slimmest
51. more precise

L E S S O N

8 ▶ Adverbs

LESSON SUMMARY

Degrees of comparison can be tricky, as can distinguishing between adjectives and adverbs. Learn which is which, and why.

dverbs are also called modifiers. Whereas adjectives modify nouns, adverbs most frequently modify verbs. They can also modify adjectives and even other adverbs.

An adverb answers four specific questions about the word it is modifying: *where?* (*here, inside, there, across, out*), *when?* (*never, tomorrow, afterward, before, while*), *how?* (*irritatingly, swiftly, suspiciously, fervently*), and *to what extent?* (*so, very, too, extremely, really*).

Memorizing these questions will help you identify adverbs. You can also look for *-ly* words that end in *-ly*, as long as you remember that not all such words are adverbs. For example, *friendly, neighborly, costly, ugly, burly, lovely,* and *cowardly* are adjectives, not adverbs.

The following table contains examples of adverb usage. For clarification, the adverbs are boldfaced and the words being modified are underlined.

ADVERBS MODIFY . . .		
Verbs	Some trains **always** <u>run</u> on time.	Margaret <u>answered</u> **quickly**.
Adjectives	. . . a **really** <u>tough</u> professor	. . . a **rather** <u>suspicious</u> character.
Other Adverbs	. . . spoke **so** <u>eloquently</u>	. . . argues **very** <u>effectively</u>

Practice

Identify the common adverbs in the following sentences.

1. I saw a hang glider floating exceptionally high over the canyon today.

2. Someday I plan to travel and sightsee throughout Europe.

3. Taking vitamins daily is one way to stay relatively healthy.

4. The kittens romped playfully around the yard and then slept soundly.

5. The Miller family skis only in the Pocono Mountains during the winter.

► Comparative Adverbs

Just as adjectives can show degrees of comparison, so can adverbs, with the use of the words *more*, *most*, *less*, and *least*, and the suffixes *-er* and *-est*. The comparative degree is used when two words are being compared; the superlative degree is used when comparing three or more.

Rule 1. One-syllable adverbs use the *-er* and *-est* endings.

Example:
fast—faster—fastest

Rule 2. Two-syllable adverbs use *more* and *most* to enhance the degree, or *less* and *least* to decrease the degree.

Examples:
quickly—more quickly—most quickly
often—less often—least often

Rule 3. Irregular adverbs do not follow either form.

Examples:
well—better—best
much—more—most

Absolute adverbs—words like *all*, *every*, *completely*, and *entirely*—already refer to everything possible, and therefore cannot be intensified any further. Similarly, *never* and *always*, two extremes of *when*, would be difficult to use in the comparative and superlative.

Practice

Determine which form of the adverb best completes each of the following sentences.

6. Jessica is the (nice, nicer, nicest) person in the office.

7. Ordering only the (low, lower, lowest)-priced items isn't always the best deal.

8. Ian works out daily and is (strong, stronger, strongest) than the rest of us.

9. Writing an old-fashioned letter may take (long, longer, longest), but it is (personal, more personal, personaler) than a simple e-mail.

10. Oscar was (less, lesser, least) grumpy after his nap.

▶ Distinguishing between Adverbs and Adjectives

It is not unusual to encounter words that look like they are one part of speech when in fact they are playing the role of another.

Examples:
The bird arrived **early** and caught the worm.
The **early** bird catches the worm.

In the first sentence, *early* is an adverb modifying the verb *arrived*, answering the question *when did the bird arrive?*—it arrived *early*. In the second sentence, *early* is an adjective modifying the noun *bird*, answering the question *what kind of bird is it?*—an *early* bird.

The following table gives some examples of adverbs and adjectives that share the same form. The adverbs and adjectives are boldfaced, and the words being modified are underlined.

Some adjectives and adverbs can be a bit troublesome because they appear interchangeable, but are not.

ADVERBS AND ADJECTIVES THAT SHARE THE SAME FORM	
ADJECTIVE	**ADVERB**
His <u>bike</u> is **fast**.	He <u>pedals</u> **fast**.
The paper contained only a **straight** <u>line</u>.	You must <u>go</u> **straight** home.
Close <u>friends</u> are a treasure.	Brian and Theresa <u>sat</u> **close** together.
Marcia keeps her **daily** <u>routine</u> simple.	<u>Exercising</u> **daily** is good for your heart.
Other words that fall into this category are *high*, *late*, *far*, *hard*, *long*, *low*, *right*, *wrong*, and *wide*.	

Good and *Well*

The word *good* is *always* an adjective. *Good* implies *satisfactory or commendable*.

> **Examples:**
> You did a **good** <u>job</u> as PR rep.
> John is such a **good** map <u>reader</u>.

Well can be an adjective *or* an adverb. As an adverb, it implies *how something is done*.

> **Examples:**
> The team <u>played</u> **well** this season.
> Katelyn can <u>swim</u> freestyle **well**.

As an adjective, *well* is used with a linking verb and usually refers to someone's health.

> **Examples:**
> Julia <u>looked</u> **well** enough to go back to school this morning.
> Our cat <u>seems</u> **well** after the successful surgery.

Bad and *Badly*

Bad is always an adjective, so it can only modify a noun or a pronoun after a linking verb.

> **Examples:**
> That <u>cough</u> of yours sounds pretty **bad**.
> The <u>cream</u> seems **bad**, so throw it out.

Badly, on the other hand, is an adverb, and can only modify an action verb. It tells *how something is done*.

> **Examples:**
> The clown <u>performs</u> magic **badly**.
> My little brother <u>behaved</u> **badly** at dinner.

Most and *Almost*

Most can be an adjective when it refers to an amount of something.

> **Examples:**
> **Most** <u>cars</u> run solely on gasoline.
> It seems that **most** <u>owners</u> agreed.

Or it can be an adverb when it is used to form the superlative degree of an adjective in a sentence.

> **Examples:**
> They were the **most** <u>surprised</u>.
> This is the **most** <u>intelligent</u> dog I've ever seen.

Almost, on the other hand, is an adverb that modifies the adjectives *every* and *all*, and the adverbs *always* and *never* in a sentence. *Almost* can also be placed before a main verb as an indication of degree.

> **Examples:**
>
> | | |
> |---|---|
> | Adjectives | Amy has **almost every** album the Beatles ever recorded. |
> | | Christian ate **almost all** of the ice cream in one sitting. |
> | Adverbs | They **almost always** participate in the annual softball game. |
> | | He **almost never** leaves without saying good-bye. |
> | Verbs | She is **almost** finished with her painting. |

Practice

Determine whether the boldfaced words in the following sentences are adjectives or adverbs.

11. I have never seen a race horse run so **fast**.

12. You should act **fast** if you want to take advantage of this **most** generous deal.

13. His **past** behavior is probably a **good** indication of what you can expect this year.

14. The parade moved **past** the judges' table at a fairly consistent pace.

15. Bear left at the fork up ahead and turn **right** at the light.

16. "You're **right**, I didn't realize how **badly** I needed that!" replied Cory.

17. His **wide** grin told me he had something up his sleeve.

18. "Open your mouth **wide** so I can see how **well** your throat is," said Dr. Angart.

19. The **far** side of the table had **almost** every dessert you could imagine.

20. It is too **bad** he has to travel so **far** to find a decent cup of coffee.

► Answers

1. exceptionally
2. Someday, throughout
3. daily, relatively
4. playfully, soundly
5. only
6. nicest
7. lowest
8. stronger
9. longer, more personal
10. less
11. adverb
12. adverb, adjective
13. adjective, adjective
14. adverb
15. adverb
16. adjective, adverb
17. adjective
18. adverb, adjective
19. adjective, adverb
20. adjective, adverb

9 ▶ Prepositions

LESSON SUMMARY

What's an OOP and where are they found? Find out in this lesson.

ike an adverb, a **preposition** conveys a relationship, usually of time (when) or place (where), between certain words in a sentence. A **prepositional phrase** is a small group of words that begins with a preposition and ends with a noun or pronoun. The noun or pronoun at the end of the phrase is called the **object of the preposition.**

Examples:
   across town
   beyond the realm **of** understanding
   under the guise **of** reality
   upon your approval
   according to the polls

COMMON PREPOSITIONS

about	above	across	after	against	along
among	around	as	at	before	behind
below	beneath	beside	between	beyond	but
by	concerning	despite	down	during	except
for	from	in	into	like	near
next	of	off	on	onto	out
outside	over	past	since	through	throughout
to	toward	under	underneath	unlike	until
up	upon	with	within	without	

The following compound prepositions are found in our speech as well:

prior to	next to	on top of	because of	in addition to
in place of	according to	in front of	on account of	aside from

Practice

Identify the prepositional phrases in the following sentences.

1. The couple rollerbladed around the park along the sidewalk, all the while being careful to avoid pedestrians.

2. Without Kyle, the cross-country just wasn't going to be the same.

3. The directions said to draw a line through any words that would cause confusion or misunderstanding.

4. Frances found her lost sneakers behind the sofa in the living room.

5. The three of us divvied up the remaining containers of chocolate pudding.

▶ Distinguishing between Prepositions and Adverbs

How can we tell whether a word is a preposition rather than an adverb? Because it begins a prepositional phrase and must always begin one. If it does not, it's an adverb. For example, in the following sentence the word *before* is an adverb because it does not begin a phrase; it stands by itself and is not followed by a noun.

I have never seen that person **before**.

In the following sentence, though, *before* is a preposition because it is followed by a noun, creating a prepositional phrase.

She stood **before** the judge to make her plea.

We sometimes encounter sentences ending with prepositions. Some are grammatically correct, while others are not. All it takes to tell the difference is to reword the sentence using the same words. If it makes sense, it is fine. If it doesn't, it is grammatically incorrect.

Example:

Crime is something I worry about.

Reworded:

Something I worry about is crime. (Grammatically correct)

Example:

It is a problem I need help with.

Reworded:

A problem I need help with is it. (Grammatically incorrect)

Remedy:

It is a problem with which I need help.

Sometimes it is awkward to reword a sentence ending with a preposition.

Example:

Indicate which person you are talking about.

Becomes:

Indicate about which person you are talking.

Example:

She brought her brushes to paint with.

Becomes:

She brought her brushes with which to paint.

You may have heard or been taught that a sentence should never end in a preposition. In modern English, however, this rule has been relaxed so as to avoid awkward constructions. Nowadays the tendency is to use your discretion in such a situation, and go with what feels right.

Practice

Determine whether the boldfaced word is a preposition or an adverb.

6. The couple walked **beside** the river **during** the afternoon.

7. It is important that you be here **before** five.

8. The presentation was done **by** Bret, Tom, and John.

9. Don't forget to set your feelings **aside** and try to be neutral.

10. We are just getting **by without** the help **of** his income.

11. As I told you **before**, it is important that the pool be cleaned regularly.

12. Tad stood **up** and clapped loudly.

13. Run **across** the street and tell your sister to come home **for** dinner.

14. **Since** last Tuesday, we have eaten **at** the diner three times.

15. The clown spun the plates **around on** his finger.

▶ Answers

1. around the park, along the sidewalk
2. Without Kyle
3. through words
4. behind the sofa, in the living room
5. of us, of pudding
6. **beside:** preposition; **during:** preposition
7. **before:** preposition
8. **by:** preposition
9. **aside:** adverb
10. **by:** adverb; **without:** preposition; **of:** preposition
11. **before:** adverb
12. **up:** adverb
13. **across:** preposition; **for:** preposition
14. **Since:** preposition; **at:** preposition
15. **around:** adverb; **on:** preposition

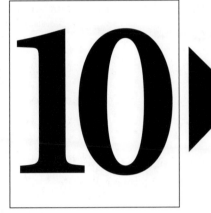

Misplaced Modifiers and Tricky Words

LESSON SUMMARY

Learn to manage those bothersome squinting, split, dangling, and disruptive modifiers that rear their heads when you least expect it.

▶ Misplaced Modifiers

When you write, you transfer what you think—what you mean to say—onto paper for someone else to read. *You* know what you mean to say, but sometimes your message can become unclear to your reader because of pesky **misplaced modifiers**: phrases or clauses that are misplaced in the sentence.

One simple way to keep a modifier from being misplaced is to keep it as close as possible to the word it modifies.

Dangling Modifiers

A **dangling modifier** does just that: It dangles, and doesn't seem to be modifying any word in particular.

Examples:
After burning dinner, Russell opened the door to let the smoke out in his pajamas.

After burning dinner in his pajamas, Russell opened the door to let the smoke out.

Both sentences make it sound as though Russell cooked dinner inside his pajamas, burned the dinner, and opened the door to air out his pajamas.

This error is easily corrected by placing the prepositional phrase *in his pajamas* closer to the word it's modifying (*Russell*), and placing the adverb phrase *after burning dinner* later in the sentence.

Corrected:
In his pajamas, Russell opened the door after burning dinner to let the smoke out.

Russell, in his pajamas, opened the door to let the smoke out after he burned dinner.

Squinting Modifiers

A modifier that is ambiguous because of its placement so that it seems to describe something on either side of it is called a **squinting modifier**.

Example:
Ryan's teacher, Ms. Bennett, told him when he completed his test to pass out some papers for her.

Did Ms. Bennett tell Ryan she wanted him to complete his test before passing out some papers for her? Or had Ryan already finished his test when Ms. Bennett told him to help her pass out papers?

Corrected:
When he completed his test, Ryan's teacher, Ms. Bennett, asked him to pass out some papers.

Ryan's teacher, Ms. Bennett, told him once he completed his test, he could pass out some papers.

Split Infinitives

Infinitives are *to* verbs, and modifiers do not belong between the two words.

Incorrect: My mom told me **to** never **lie**.
Corrected: My mom told me never **to lie**.

Disruptive Modifiers

When a modifying clause is improperly placed within a sentence, it disrupts the flow of the words.

Example:
I will not tolerate, just because you're the star, your disrespectful outbursts.

Corrected:
I will not tolerate your disrespectful outbursts just because you're the star.

Managing Your Modifiers

Here are a few rules to help you place modifiers correctly in a sentence.

Rule 1. Place simple adjectives before the nouns they are modifying.

Example:
Wearing a **green** raincoat, the exhausted student walked home in the rain.

Rule 2. Place adjective phrases and adjective clauses after the nouns being modified.

Example:
The surfer **with long blond hair** rode the ten-foot wave with ease.

Rule 3. Place *only*, *barely*, *just*, and *almost* before the noun or verb being modified. Their placement determines the message in your sentence.

Examples:
Only Peter ran to the store. [No one else but Peter went.]
Peter **only** ran to the store. [He didn't walk.]
Peter ran **only** to the store. [He didn't go anywhere else.]
Peter ran to the **only** store. [There was no other store around but that one.]
Peter ran to the store **only**. [He ran to the store, and did nothing else.]

Practice
Rewrite each sentence so that the modifiers are properly placed.

1. While fixing the broken lamp, our dog began to bark ferociously.

2. Gladys sang with the choir with a broken leg.

3. Sara played the Sonata in G for her guests on the piano.

4. Covered in sauce, I saw a man barbequing on my bike.

5. Holding hands and admiring the view, the birds chirped and the butterflies fluttered.

▶ Tricky Words

As you've noticed, words in the English language can be tricky! Homonyms and homographs remind us that not only should we know how to spell words correctly, but sometimes we need to know which correct spelling of a word is the one we want.

Homonyms
Homonyms are words that are pronounced exactly same even though they are spelled differently. See the following table for some familiar examples.

HOMONYMS

ad/add	I clipped the **ad** in the newspaper. **Add** the items up to get the total.
allowed/aloud	No one is **allowed** in my office without permission. I heard him read my name **aloud** today.
ant/aunt	I saw an **ant** carry a crumb up the table leg. **Aunt** Myrtle is eccentric.
ate/eight	Dad **ate** a rack of ribs at dinner. There are **eight** people in my family.
bare/bear	Old Mother Hubbard's cupboard was **bare**. **Bear** hunting is illegal in some states.
blew/blue	Linda **blew** her birthday candles out. One **blue** sock was missing.
brake/break	Tap the **brake** gently when stopping in snow. Give me a **break**, please.
buy/by	Can you **buy** milk on your way home? They quickly ran **by** the store.
cent/scent/sent	One **cent** is called a penny. I recognized the **scent** of her perfume immediately. Greg **sent** flowers to Dahlia on Mother's Day.
chews/choose	My dog **chews** on almost anything. May I **choose** the next game to play?
colonel/kernel	Grandpa Jim was a **colonel** in the Navy. Don't bite on the popcorn **kernel**.
dear/deer	She is such a **dear** friend. **Deer** roam the woods beside my house.
dew/do/due	The morning **dew** felt cold on my feet. I **do** not like licorice. The first payment is **due** in four days.
ewe/yew/you	The **ewe** watched her lamb closely. A small evergreen called a **yew** is prevalent on most continents. I love **you**.
flew/flu/flue	They **flew** to Orlando for the first time. It is not easy to catch the **flu**. The chimney **flue** was dirty.

HOMONYMS *(Continued)*	
flour/flower	**Flour** is used to make many desserts.
	The **flower** lasted only four days in the vase.
heal/heel/he'll	Wounds **heal** at different rates.
	Her **heel** hurt after she took her new shoe off.
	He'll be the best choice, I think.
hear/here	Can you **hear** well?
	Here are the apples from the basket.
hole/whole	The **hole** they dug was three feet deep.
	I can't believe I ate the **whole** sandwich.
hour/our	Within the next **hour**, you will see a real difference.
	Our friends are moving in September.
aisle/isle/I'll	The grocery **aisle** was messy and chaotic.
	They bought a small **isle** in the Gulf of Mexico.
	I'll show you how to do this.
knew/new	He **knew** better than to do that.
	Our **new** neighbors built a deck.
knot/not	I tried to untie the **knot** in her shoestring.
	They could **not** see because of the fog.
know/no	I **know** how to jog backward.
	No, he doesn't.
meat/meet	The **meat** at her butcher shop is fresh.
	Let's **meet** next week to finish this.
need/kneed/knead	I **need** a vacation, do you?
	Nathan got **kneed** in the side by his opponent.
	You must **knead** the bread dough before letting it rise.
one/won	Eileen has **one** more hour of work left.
	Ashley wished she had **won** the prize.
pair/pear	Hillary's **pair** of shoes was two sizes too small.
	Baked **pear** is easy to make.
peak/peek/pique	We stood at the **peak** of the mountain in awe.
	He took a quick **peek** in her shopping bag.
	What I overhead **piqued** my curiosity.
principal/principle	The **principal** idea is to help others.
	It's the **principle** of the matter, and nothing else.

(Continued)

HOMONYMS *(Continued)*	
rain/reign/rein	Will it **rain** again tomorrow?
	King Henry VIII's **reign** over England lasted 38 years.
	The horse's **rein** was worn and needed replacing.
right/rite/write	You're **right**; turn **right** at the light up ahead.
	The tribe's **rite** of passage involved marriage.
	Teachers often ask students to **write** essays.
sail/sale	Jan will **sail** in the Caribbean for one week.
	I bought the living room furniture on **sale**.
scene/seen	**Scene** four in the play was the turning point in the plot.
	I have never **seen** an octopus before.
stationary/stationery	The guard stood **stationary** for several hours.
	The pink **stationery** had her monogram on it.
there/their/they're	**There** is an outside chance that we can go.
	It took **their** bus 18 hours to get home.
	They're supposed to confirm the appointment.
threw/through	The child **threw** a tantrum in the middle of the store.
	Through thick and thin, the friends remained loyal.
to/too/two	I will try **to** change this light bulb with one hand.
	He plays video games **too** often.
	My **two** sisters look alike.
wood/would	Pile the **wood** by the back of the shed.
	Would you care to give me a hand?
which/witch	**Which** sneaker you choose is solely up to you.
	Dorothy outsmarted the wicked **witch** in her own castle.
weather/whether	The **weather** could be severe, so be cautious.
	I can't decide **whether** to stay or leave.
who's/whose	**Who's** going to Albany with Craig tomorrow?
	Is this **whose** coat you thought it would be?

Homographs

Homographs are words that are spelled exactly the same but have completely different meanings. Following are some familiar examples.

HOMOGRAPHS	
address	You should **address** the envelope with the **address** on the label.
bass	He is now a **bass** fisherman, even though he plays the **bass** in a rock band.
bow	I was asked to **bow** to the king and remove my **bow** and arrows.
close	My manager will **close** up tonight; luckily he lives **close** by.
conflict	The reports **conflict** about the recent **conflict** in Congress.
desert	The solider did not **desert** his unit stationed in the **desert**.
does	He **does** see the **does** standing off to the side of the road.
dove	The **dove dove** toward the flock of gulls to defend his mate.
house	The **house** around the corner will **house** your dog for you while you're away.
lead	He had finally taken the **lead** in the crossword competition when the **lead** on his pencil broke.
live	I **live** next to the arena, so I'll see many concerts **live**.
minute	The **minute** I saw her, she hounded me about the most **minute** details to the contract.
number	The greater **number** of popsicles I ate, the **number** my tongue became.
present	To **present** this special **present** to the winner was an honor.
produce	Many farms **produce produce** during the summer.
read	I will **read** the same book you **read** last summer.
record	Don't forget to **record** his high-jump **record** in the books.
resume	Let's **resume** updating your **resume** tomorrow.
separate	**Separate** your socks by color and place them in a **separate** drawer in your dresser.
tear	"Don't **tear** my book!" the little girl said with a **tear** in her eye.
use	I don't have any **use** for this, so feel free to **use** it!
wind	With the **wind** so strong, I couldn't **wind** the string of the kite easily.
wound	He **wound** up wrapping his **wound** with gauze.

Usually, homographs are pronounced differently, depending on their meaning, but sometimes they can even sound the same.

pine	I **pine** for the **pine** trees of my native Black Forest.
well	I didn't feel **well** after drinking the water from the **well**.

Practice

Look at each pair of clues to determine the words they suggest. Then indicate whether they are homonyms or homographs.

6. to move through the air/a pesky insect: homonym/homograph

7. a fish/a low tone: homonym/homograph

8. consumed/a number: homonym/homograph

9. to make/fruits and vegetables: homonym/homograph

10. permitted/audible: homonym/homograph

11. small/one-sixtieth of an hour: homonym/homograph

12. to bend at the waist/a large branch: homonym/homograph

13. uppercase/place of state government: homonym/homograph

14. also/deuce: homonym/homograph

15. still/writing paper: homonym/homograph

16. something in a package/satisfied: homonym/homograph

17. yeast, water, and flour mass/a female deer: homonym/homograph

18. next to/to shut: homonym/homograph

19. correct/a ceremony: homonym/homograph

20. discounted price/to steer a small boat: homonym/homograph

21. to purchase/by means of: homonym/homograph

22. odor/transmitted: homonym/homograph

23. gnaws/select: homonym/homograph

24. guide/heavy metal: homonym/homograph

25. a brief look/to stimulate: homonym/homograph

▶ Answers

Here are possible answers for questions 1–5. (Some answers may vary.)

1. While I was fixing the broken lamp, our dog began to bark ferociously.
2. Gladys, who had a broken leg, sang with the choir.
3. Sara played the Sonata in G on the piano for her guests.
4. While riding my bike, I saw a man covered in sauce and barbequing.
5. As we held hands and admired the view, the birds chirped and the butterflies fluttered.
6. **fly/fly**: homograph
7. **bass/bass**: homograph
8. **ate/eight**: homonym
9. **produce/produce**: homograph
10. **allowed/aloud**: homonym
11. **minute/minute**: homograph
12. **bow/bough**: homonym
13. **capital/capitol**: homonym
14. **too/two**: homonym
15. **stationary/stationery**: homonym
16. **content/content**: homograph
17. **dough/doe**: homonym
18. **close/close**: homograph
19. **right/rite**: homonym
20. **sale/sail**: homonym
21. **buy/by**: homonym
22. **scent/sent**: homonym
23. **chews/choose**: homonym
24. **lead/lead**: homograph
25. **peek/pique**: homonym

Sentence Structure

11 ▶ Sentence Basics

LESSON SUMMARY
Basic sentence structure goes far beyond subjects and predicates.
Learn how complements come into play.

The fundamental component of speech and writing, sentences help people communicate and make themselves understood to others. Every complete sentence is made up of two major components— a **subject**—a noun or pronoun that tells us *whom* or *what* the sentence is about, and a **predicate**— a verb that tells us what the subject is *doing* or what *condition* the subject is in.

▶ Subjects

Finding the subject of a sentence is as simple as asking *who?* or *what?* in relation to the verb. In the following examples, the subject is underlined <u>once</u> and the verb is underlined <u>twice</u>.

A subject can be a proper noun:

      S   V

<u>Thomas</u> <u>updates</u> his resume regularly.

Who updates? **Thomas**; thus, <u>Thomas</u> is the subject.

A subject can be a common noun:

      S   V

The real estate <u>market</u> <u>fluctuates</u> yearly.

What fluctuates? The **market**; thus, <u>market</u> is the subject.

A subject can be a pronoun:

      S   V

<u>They</u> <u>traveled</u> overseas for the meeting.

Who traveled? **They** did; thus, <u>They</u> is the subject.

A subject can be compound (two or more nouns playing an equal role in the sentence):

  S   S   V

<u>Books</u> and the <u>Internet</u> <u>contain</u> helpful information.

What contain? **Books** and the **Internet**; thus, <u>books</u> and <u>Internet</u> play the role equally as the subject.

Although the subject is typically found at the beginning of the sentence, it can also appear elsewhere in the sentence.

In the middle:
Before lunch, <u>Michelle</u> <u>decided</u> to run quickly to the bank.

At the end:
At the end of the pier <u>sat</u> the lone <u>fisherman</u>.

Tricky Subjects
Not all sentences have an obvious, or stated, noun, or pronoun as a subject; sometimes the subject is implied. Imperative sentences (sentences that make a request or a command) always have an implied subject:

Wash your hands frequently during the day to prevent colds.

If you ask yourself **who** or **what** <u>wash</u>? there isn't a noun in the sentence that can act as the answer. That is because the subject is *implied*; that subject is the pronoun **you**:

(<u>You</u>) <u>wash</u> your hands frequently during the day to prevent colds.

To find the subject in a question, turn the question into a statement that places the subject before the verb:

Did Ed go to the convention in Seattle, or not?

becomes:

<u>Ed</u> <u>went</u> to the convention in Seattle.

You can then ask yourself **Who** <u>went</u>? **Ed** is your subject.

Practice

Identify the simple subject in the following sentences.

1. Yesterday, we lost electricity for 16 hours.

2. Several crocodiles were found in the pond at the park.

3. Gail should make an effort to call her grandfather more often.

4. Weren't dachshunds bred for hunting the burrow-dwelling badger?

5. The hammock was his favorite place to relax.

6. I usually park my car in the garage across the street.

7. Keith brought the boat to the island marina.

8. Some raw vegetables taste great in salads.

9. Place some paper clips from the drawer in my desk into the container, please.

10. This new recipe for Key lime pie is a success!

▶ Predicates

Predicates tell something about the subject or subjects in a sentence. The verb, known as the **simple predicate**, expresses the action done by or to the subject, or tells about its condition. You can find the simple predicate in a sentence by asking yourself what word indicates action being done by or to the subject or conveys the condition of the subject.

Examples:

S   V

She approached her supervisor about her recent performance review.

S

The itinerary for Joseph's business trip

V

was changed.

S   V

Meghan was energetic and results-driven.

Like subjects, predicates can be single or compound, which means that there are two or more verbs that relate to the same subject or compound subject in the sentence.

Examples:

S   V   V   V

At practice, we stretch, run, drill, and

V

scrimmage.

S   S   V

Last Monday, George and Marty arrived late and

V

ran two extra laps.

Practice

Identify the simple predicate in the following sentences.

11. The thunderstorm's wind was severe and caused the blackout.

12. A jogger spotted the large reptiles lurking in the mud and called the police.

13. After dinner, Grandpa hinted that he has missed hearing all about her travels.

14. Rabbit, raccoon, and fox, also burrow-dwellers, are hunted by dachshunds as well.

15. Phil's hammock was stretched between two large oaks: It was the perfect place for napping.

16. Street-side parking in this congested area is simply out of the question.

17. He rented the 30-foot boat slip for $210 per month.

18. Common salad vegetables are spinach, carrots, broccoli, cucumber, and tomato.

19. The stapler on the file cabinet might also need refilling.

20. Key limes differ from other limes in their small round shape and acidic taste.

► Complements

The purpose of good communication is to get your message across clearly to your listener or speaker. Sometimes a sentence is complete with just a subject and a verb:

> Stanley left.
> Please be quiet.
> What's up?
> How are you?

Other sentences require more information to complete their meaning:

> Kyle picked _____.
> Gina took _____.

The additional parts that these sentences require are called **complements**.

Examples:
> Kyle picked Andrew first.
> Gina took a breath.

The complements *Andrew* and *breath* complete the meaning in these sentences by telling us *what* the subjects *picked* and *took*. Complements can include direct objects, indirect objects, predicate nouns, and predicate adjectives.

Direct and Indirect Objects

A **direct object** is a complement that is used in a sentence with an *action verb*. It is a noun or pronoun that is "directly" related with the action verb and receives the action from that verb. Direct objects answer **whom?** or **what?** about the action verb.

Examples:

          S   V   D.O.
> Kyle picked Andrew first.   Picked whom?
                                    Andrew.

              S   V   D.O.
> Gina took a breath.   Took what? a *breath*

Like subjects and predicates, direct objects can also be **compound**, meaning that one or more verbs can share more than one direct object.

Example:

                                      S   V
> Wanda, a successful real estate agent, listed and
>   V   D.O.   D.O.
> sold a house and a farm this week.

Note: All sentences must have a subject, but not all sentences require an object.

A sentence that has a direct object can also have an **indirect object**. Because an indirect object tells which person or thing is the recipient of the direct object, you cannot have an indirect object without a direct object. You can easily identify a direct object by asking yourself *to or for whom?* or *to or for what?* after an action verb. Indirect objects are usually found between the verb and the direct object.

Example:

                S   V   I.O.
> The car salesperson showed Chris the latest
                          D.O.
> Mustang GT model.

Practice
Identify the direct and indirect object (if any) in the following sentences.

21. I took the milk and the meat from my broken refrigerator and placed them into a cooler.

22. The wildlife conservation officer captured and took them to the local zoo.

23. Gail wrote her grandfather a long and detailed letter instead.

24. Dachshunds find burrows and dens with their keen sense of smell.

25. Phil brought a newspaper with him so he could read, too.

26. Many cars get dents and scratches because other drivers are careless.

27. Sandbar marinas rent residents their slips year-round.

28. Chef Williams gave me a delicious recipe for hot bacon dressing.

29. Janine offered the helpful student a piece of candy for his efforts.

30. Columbus brought Hispaniola the Key lime in the 1500s.

Predicate Nouns and Predicate Adjectives

Known as **subject complements**, predicate nouns rename the subject and predicate adjectives or describe the subject. They are found in sentences with linking verbs, not action verbs.

When a predicate noun follows a linking verb, the linking verb acts like an equals sign (=):

$$\begin{array}{ccc} \text{S} & \text{V} & \text{P.N.} \end{array}$$
DeVaughn is the |coach|.   **means**
    DeVaughn = the coach.

Predicate nouns can also be compound in form, so long as they are identifying the same noun:

$$\begin{array}{cccc} \text{S} & \text{V} & \text{P.N.} & \text{P.N.} \end{array}$$
Carla was |professor| and |mentor| to many
    students.

Predicate adjectives also follow a linking verb and describe or modify the subject:

$$\begin{array}{ccc} \text{S} & \text{V} & \text{P.A.} \end{array}$$
The child grew |distraught| after her mother left
    the daycare center.

Predicate adjectives can be compound in form, as well:

$$\begin{array}{ccc} \text{S} & \text{V} & \text{P.A.} \end{array}$$
Following the interview, Bill felt |excited| and
    P.A.
|optimistic|.

Practice

Identify the predicate nouns and predicate adjectives in the following sentences.

31. The milk stayed cold and fresh in the ice-filled cooler.

32. The crocodiles became new members of the reptile exhibit.

33. As a young man, Grandfather was a sailor and traveled the world.

34. Dachshunds are short-legged dogs, sometimes referred to as "wiener dogs" because of their sausage-shaped bodies.

35. Canvas hammocks became popular with the English Navy in the 1600s.

36. Parking spaces in any large city can be difficult to find.

37. Slips are docking spaces for boats.

38. Salads are healthy with the right kind of dressing.

39. Janine is a middle school teacher in Muncie, Indiana.

40. Key limes are popular in drinks, desserts, and marinades.

▶ Answers

1. we
2. crocodiles
3. Gail
4. dachshunds
5. hammock
6. I
7. Keith
8. vegetables
9. (you)
10. recipe
11. was, caused
12. spotted, called
13. hinted
14. are hunted
15. was stretched
16. is
17. rented
18. are
19. might need
20. differ
21. direct object: **milk**, **meat**, **them**; indirect object: none
22. direct object: **them**; indirect object: none
23. direct object: **letter**; indirect object: **grandfather**
24. direct object: **burrows**, **dens**; indirect object: none
25. direct object: **newspaper**; indirect object: none
26. direct object: **dents**, **scratches**; indirect object: none
27. direct object: **slips**; indirect object: **residents**
28. direct object: **recipe**; indirect object: **me**
29. direct object: **candy**; indirect object: **student**
30. direct object: **Key lime**; indirect object: **Hispaniola**
31. predicate noun: none; predicate adjective: **cold**, **fresh**
32. predicate noun: **members**; predicate adjective: none
33. predicate noun: **sailor**; predicate adjective: none
34. predicate noun: **dogs**; predicate adjective: none
35. predicate noun: none; predicate adjective: **popular**
36. predicate noun: none; predicate adjective: **difficult**
37. predicate noun: **spaces**; predicate adjective: none
38. predicate noun: none; predicate adjective: **healthy**
39. predicate noun: **teacher**; predicate adjective: none
40. predicate noun: none; predicate adjective: **popular**

LESSON

12 ▶ Agreement

LESSON SUMMARY

Agreement between subjects and verbs and between antecedents and their pronouns is essential. Learn whether to use a singular or plural verb with compound subjects and indefinite pronouns.

▶ Subject-Verb Agreement

Subjects and verbs must always be compatible in number and person. A singular subject, referring to only one person, place, or thing, must be coupled with a singular verb. Likewise, plural subjects (referring to more than one) will take a plural verb.

Singular:	*Shirley* **wants** to buy a new car.	She **is** shopping for one now.
	Rex usually **plays** catch with me.	He **was** not feeling well today.
Plural:	*Trish* and *Dot* **run** errands together.	They **are** at the supermarket.
	Sandy, *Alexa*, and *I* **discuss** books.	We **were** hoping to meet today.

Notice the endings of the singular and the plural verbs. Unlike nouns, third-person singular verbs end in *-s*, while the plural verbs do not.

Verbs move sentences along. We are able to tell *when* events happen simply by considering the tense of the verb in a sentence. Because many verbs are so easily recognizable, they come across as exceptionally harsh to our ears when they are used improperly. This is espe-cially true of the most widely used verb form in the English language—the verb *be*. The following table shows how the verb *be* is conjugated according to number, form, and person (s̲ingular or p̲lural, first, second, third person).

	SUBJECT	PRESENT	PAST
First/S	I	am	was
Second/S & P	you	are	were
Third/S	he, she, it	is	was
First/P	we	are	were
Third/P	they	are	were

It is interesting to note that the conjugated forms of the verb *be* don't include the word *be* at all. For reference, the nonparticipial forms of the verb *be* are as follows: *am, is, are, was, were*.

That being said, it is not unusual to hear *be* used as a verb in casual language—albeit it is used improperly. You should note that *be never follows a subject in a sentence without a helping verb*.

Incorrect:
I **be** taking the mail to the post office this morning.
They **be** cooking dinner, and we **be** washing the dishes.

Correct:
I **am** taking the mail to the post office this morning.
They **are** cooking dinner, and we **are** washing the dishes.

Practice
Identify the verb that correctly agrees with the subject in each sentence.

1. Brian (attend, attends) classes at Rutgers University this semester.

2. Steve and Ed (borrow, borrows) money all the time and never pay me back.

3. They (likes, like) the hamburgers at this restaurant more than those at the other.

4. Each year, one can see many birds (fly, flies) south for the winter.

5. When it is cold, the children (watch, watches) the waves from the shore instead.

Compound Subjects and Verbs
When two or more subjects share the same verb, you have what is called a **compound subject**. The conjunctions *and*, *or*, or *nor* are used to connect compound subjects together.

Example:
Pink and black **are** traditional ballet colors.

When the conjunction *and* is used, the subjects are looked at as equals, so the verb used will be plural. An exception to this rule is when the subjects are thought of as a single unit, such as *spaghetti and meatballs*, or *macaroni and cheese*.

When singular subjects are joined by the conjunction *or* or *nor*, each subject is considered a separate unit, so the verb used will be *singular*. When plural subjects are joined by *or* or *nor*, the verb used will be *plural*, since each of the subjects is plural.

Singular:

Green or yellow squash **is** used in this recipe.

Neither the chair nor the table **has** any scratches.

Plural:

Coaches or managers may attend the monthly team meetings.

Neither parents nor spectators would likely be interested in attending.

If you have a sentence that uses a singular and a plural subject, it may be hard to decide whether to use a singular or a plural verb. But the solution is very simple: Whichever subject you mention last in the sentence, whether singular or plural, will determine the correct verb to use:

Either *pancakes or cereal* **is** available for breakfast today.

Either *cereal or pancakes* **are** available for breakfast today.

Practice

Identify the verb that correctly completes the following sentences.

6. Neither Bob nor Joe (read, reads) the newspaper in the morning.

7. Janice and Jackie (commute, commutes) to the city by train.

8. Peanut butter and jelly (is, are) my daughter's favorite lunch.

9. Either Danielle or Veronica (is, are) likely to be chosen for first place.

10. Neither spaghetti nor meatballs (is, are) found on the menu.

▶ Pronoun Subjects and Verbs

Indefinite pronouns, such as *everyone, both, few,* and *all,* are very general when referring to people, places, or things. Because we are concerned with subjects and verbs agreeing in number, it is easy to tell whether most indefinite pronouns are singular or plural, with only a handful of exceptions.

INDEFINITE PRONOUNS						
SINGULAR				**PLURAL**	**BOTH**	
anybody	everybody	neither	other	both	all	some
anyone	everyone	nobody	somebody	few	any	
anything	everything	no one	someone	many	more	
each	little	nothing	something	others	most	
either	much	one		several	none	

As with any other pronoun, a singular indefinite pronoun will take a singular verb and a plural one will take a plural verb. When using pronouns that can be both singular and plural, you need to look at the noun that is being referred to by the indefinite pronoun, to help you determine what verb to use:

Most of these *peaches* **are** bruised.

Most of his *room* **is** clean.

Practice

Identify the verb that will agree with the indefinite pronouns in the following sentences.

11. Nothing (seem, seems) to bother him.

12. Most of the camera equipment (belong, belongs) to Mr. Jackson.

13. Everything in those boxes (go, goes) to the church for its tag sale.

14. Several of the cars (have, has) repairs to be made before inspection.

15. More of these pieces (were, was) found under the chair in the kitchen.

► Antecedents and Pronouns

You studied pronouns in Lesson 3, but here are some additional pronouns you need to know.

COMMON ENGLISH PRONOUNS				
all	another	any	anybody	anyone
anything	both	each	either	everybody
everyone	everything	few	he	her
hers	herself	him	himself	his
I	it	its	itself	many
me	mine	my	myself	neither
no one	nobody	none	nothing	one
others	our	ours	ourselves	she
some	somebody	someone	something	that
their	theirs	them	themselves	these
they	this	us	we	what
which	who	whom	whose	you
your	yours	yourself	yourselves	

Without pronouns, communicating even in simple sentences would be very contrived because of the necessary and constant repetition of nouns . . .

Example:
Lillian and Gina went to Florida for a long weekend of rest and relaxation. Lillian and Gina planned to meet up with Lillian and Gina's old friends Stephanie and Jean. Lillian, Gina, Stephanie, and Jean decided Lillian, Gina, Stephanie, and Jean would have lunch at Lillian, Gina, Stephanie, and Jean's old watering hole. Lillian, Gina, Stephanie, and Jean had a great time and Lillian, Gina, Stephanie, and Jean decided to have lunch at Lillian, Gina, Stephanie, and Jean's old watering hole again soon.

Pronouns are a part of speech that can (fortunately) take the place of nouns. The antecedent is the word that the pronoun replaced.

Example:

> Adel liked the new headphones she bought this afternoon.

The pronoun *she* in the sentence refers to *Adel*, so *Adel* is antecedent. Because *Adel* is one girl, the pronoun *she*

is used instead of *they*. There must be agreement as to gender, number, and person between the antecedent and its pronoun.

	Singular	**Plural**
First person:	I, me, my, mine	we, us, our
Second person:	you, your, yours	you, your, yours
Third person:	he, she, it	they, them, their

Let's see why that is not only important, but *necessary*:

> *Mrs. Parker* shopped for a pair of strappy sandals in the perfect shade of chartreuse green and yellow for his new sundress.

It is obvious that Mrs. Parker is a female, and the only appropriate possessive pronoun to agree with that would be *her*, not *his* as it says in the sentence. Try another:

> *Rosemarie* yawned and put *their* feet up to take *his* afternoon nap.

Rosemarie is tired and wants to take a nap, but the sentence has her putting someone else's feet up and, unfortunately, taking someone else's nap for them.

When a sentence has multiple subjects, pronoun ambiguity sets in for your listener or reader. With too many *he*'s, *she*'s, and *they*'s, the message can become garbled, and your audience gets lost.

Example:

> Kris told Nancy that Fran ran into Hali after she left class, and over coffee, she spilled the beans that she heard her boyfriend say that he thought she was boring.

That's confusing. Who left class? Hali or Fran or Kris? Who spilled the beans? Kris? Perhaps Fran? Could it have been Nancy? And who has the boyfriend who thinks she's boring?

Practice

Determine which pronoun best fits for pronoun-antecedent agreement in each sentence.

16. Geoff and Hank took _____ break in the lobby.

17. Everybody went to _____ tent after the bonfire.

18. Vivian reached _____ hand across the table to shake Jim's hand.

19. Both drivers checked _____ engines before approaching the starting line.

20. The bird flew to _____ nest high in the tree top.

▶ **Answers**

1. attends	**11.** seems
2. borrow	**12.** belongs
3. like	**13.** goes
4. fly	**14.** have
5. watch	**15.** were
6. reads	**16.** their
7. commute	**17.** his or her
8. is	**18.** her
9. is	**19.** their
10. are	**20.** its

LESSON

13▶ Phrases

LESSON SUMMARY

Learn how little groups of words can wear many hats in sentences. In this sentence, it's an *adjective*; in that one, it's an *adverb*; and in the other one, it's a *noun*. Find out why in this lesson.

 phrase is a group of two or more words that either express a thought or function as a particular part of speech in a sentence. Unlike clauses (see Lesson 14), phrases do not contain a subject and a predicate.

SAMPLE PHRASES	
NO PREDICATE	**NO SUBJECT**
The bicycles	goes skating often
Several	is from another planet
Our house	are missing some parts

▶ Prepositional Phrases

The **prepositional phrase** is the most common type of phrase. (For a review of prepositions, see Lesson 9.) In a sentence, a prepositional phrase can play the role of an adjective—in which case, it is called an adjective phrase—or of an adverb—in which case, it is called an adverb phrase. We also have verbal phrases (phrases that are based on verbs), which can be participial phrases, gerund phrases, or infinitive phrases, and can function as nouns, adjectives, or adverbs. Lastly, appositive phrases explain or give further detail about the word or words they are modifying.

Adjective and Adverb Phrases

A prepositional phrase, which begins with a preposition and ends with a noun or pronoun, can function like an adjective or an adverb in a sentence. Like an adjective, an adjective phrase will answer *what kind?* Or *which one?* about the noun or pronoun it is modifying. Unlike an adjective, which typically precedes the noun it modifies, the adjective phrase generally comes after the noun.

> **Example:**
> A group of friends **from work** are meeting tonight for dinner.

Here, the prepositional phrase *from work* acts like an adjective. We know that it is an adjective phrase because it modifies the noun *group* and answers the question *which one?* about the group.

Adverb phrases modify verbs, adjectives, and adverbs. An adverb phrase will answer *where? when? how?* or *to what extent?* about the word it is modifying, and usually provides more detail than a typical adverb.

> **Example:**
> We will meet **at our favorite restaurant at six o'clock.**

Here, the prepositional phrases *at our favorite restaurant* and *at six o'clock* act like adverbs, modifying the verb *meet* and answering the questions *where?* and *when?* about the meeting.

Practice

Identify the adjective and adverb phrases in the sentences below.

1. Forests with dry grass and brush burn easily.

2. The workers on the platform worked hard in the hot sun.

3. The picture in the antique frame was of my grandmother.

4. The gray squirrels scampered along the fence rail in the backyard.

5. The divers traversed through deep waters of the Caribbean.

▶ Verbal Phrases

The word *verbal* refers to words that are derived from *verbs*. The three types of verbal phrases are participial phrases—which act like adjectives—and gerund phrases and infinitive phrases—which act like nouns.

Participial Phrases

Participial phrases begin with a participle, a present tense (*-ing*) verb or a past tense (*ed, en, t,* or *n*) verb. Participial phrases act like adjectives, describing or giving more detail about nouns or pronouns in a sentence.

> **Examples:**
> **Looking hot and tired,** the gardener sat in the shade of a nearby tree.
> **Shaken by the unexpected accident,** Harry called 911 for assistance.

The present participle *looking* (*look* + *ing*), modifies the noun *gardener*. The words *hot and tired* complete the participial phrase. The phrase *Shaken by the unexpected accident* follows the same configuration, except that it is in past participle (*shake* + *n*) form.

Infinitive Phrases

Infinitive phrases begin with the word *to* plus a verb. Infinitive phrases act like nouns, adjectives, or adverbs in a sentence, depending on their function.

> **Example:**
> **To run a mile in less than six minutes** was Tommy's aim this season.

The infinitive phrase *to run a mile in less than six minutes* is functioning as a noun because it is the complete subject of the sentence.

> **Example:**
> Tommy aims **to run a mile in less than six minutes** this season.

To run a mile in less than six minutes in this sentence is also functioning as a noun because it is the direct object of the verb *aims*.

> **Example:**
> **To run a mile in less than six minutes,** Tommy trains hard this season.

To run a mile in less than six minutes in this sentence is functioning as an *adjective* because it modifies the noun *Tommy*.

> **Example:**
> Tommy is training this season **to run a mile in less than six minutes.**

To run a mile in less than six minutes in this sentence is functioning as an adverb because it modifies the verb *training*.

Gerund Phrases

Gerund phrases begin with a gerund, an *ing* verb acting as a noun. Gerund phrases always work like a noun in a sentence, so they can function as either subjects or objects.

> **Example:**
> **Tasting chocolate for a living** can be a delicious yet fattening profession.

The gerund phrase *tasting chocolate for a living* functions as a noun and is the complete subject of the sentence.

> **Example:**
> Debbie's profession is **sampling chocolate.**

The gerund phrase *sampling chocolate* functions as a noun and is the subject complement of the linking verb *is* and the subject *profession*.

> **Example:**
> Debbie enjoys **working with chocolate.**

The gerund phrase *working with chocolate* functions as a noun and is the direct object of the verb *enjoys*.

Practice

Identify the types of phrases in the sentences below.

6. *To conclude tonight's program*, our chief of staff would like to say a few words.

7. *Wanting to save money*, Lysbeth spent the morning clipping and filing coupons.

8. Marybeth dreams about *becoming a NASA astronaut.*

9. The plumber was unable *to finish the difficult job* in one day.

10. *Excusing the boys* for their rude and reckless behavior was not an option.

Appositive Phrases

An **appositive** is a word or phrase that renames, identifies, or gives more detail about a noun or pronoun that it follows in the sentence.

Example:

My brother, **a clown by profession**, works all weekend at parties and gatherings.

In this sentence, the noun *brother* is being further identified by the appositive phrase *a clown by profession.*

Practice

Identify the appositive phrases in the following sentences and the noun or pronoun they are modifying.

11. Julie, an excellent tennis player, will be going to the state finals for the Junior American Tennis Association this August.

12. The peanut, not really a nut but a legume, is a major allergen for children and adults around the world.

13. The lost bike was returned to Lawrence, the rightful owner.

14. Kilmer, a video game whiz, has a patent for a new kind of gaming system.

15. Marcie told a story about the Tasmanian devil, an urban legend.

▶ Answers

1. **with dry grass and brush:** adjective phrase
2. **on the platform:** adjective phrase; **in the hot sun:** adverb phrase
3. **in the antique frame, of my grandmother:** adjective phrases
4. **along the fence rail, in the backyard:** adverb phrases
5. **through deep waters, of the Caribbean:** adverb phrases
6. infinitive phrase
7. participial phrase
8. gerund phrase
9. infinitive phrase
10. gerund phrase
11. **an excellent tennis player** modifies *Julie*
12. **not really a nut but a legume** modifies *peanut*
13. **the rightful owner** modifies *Lawrence*
14. **a video game whiz** modifies *Kilmer*
15. **an urban legend** modifies *Tasmanian devil*

14 ▶ Clauses

LESSON SUMMARY

Like phrases, clauses also take on many different jobs—even as a sentence! See why and how in this lesson.

A **clause** differs from a phrase in that it has its own subject and verb. This allows some clauses to be sentences, either independently or within a larger sentence. A sentence might contain or even be entirely composed of as many as three or more clauses. The two kinds of clauses are **independent** and **subordinate**.

▶ Independent Clauses

Sometimes referred to as a main clause, an **independent clause** can stand alone as a simple sentence.

Examples:
You have a nice smile.
It lights up your eyes.

With the help of a semicolon or a coordinating conjunction, we can join these two independent clauses together to form a single sentence.

Examples:
You have a nice smile; it lights up your eyes.
You have a nice smile **and** it lights up your eyes.

Don't confuse the comma with the semicolon. Joining the two clauses with a comma instead of a semicolon would result in what is called a comma splice. (See Lesson 18.)

The coordinating conjunctions *and, or, for, nor, but, yet,* and *so* join the clauses together, but they don't belong to either clause if you separate them. The rule of putting a comma between the first clause and the coordinating conjunction is becoming more relaxed, especially in shorter sentences. (See Lesson 16.)

Examples:
I looked for my lost address book, **but** I could not find it.
Charlotte watered the tree every day, **for** it was new.
Hans wanted to learn how to play golf, **so** he took lessons.

Some sentences may contain as many as three or more independent clauses.

Example:
I looked for my lost address book, **but** I could not find it, **so** I decided to start a new one; I knew it would be useful.

▶ Subordinate Clauses

A **subordinate clause**, or dependent clause, also contains a subject and a verb, but it cannot stand alone as simple sentences. It depends on another clause in the sentence to help it do its job. Subordinate clauses look like independent clauses except that they can begin with a subordinating conjunction.

Examples:
before I knew it
so I don't forget it
whenever you're in town

SUBORDINATING CONJUNCTIONS				
after	although	as if	as long as	as much as
as soon as	because	before	even if	even though
if	in order that	now that	provided that	since
so	so long as	though	unless	until
when	whenever	whereas	whether	while
where				

Subordinate clauses can also begin with a relative pronoun.

Examples:
whom I saw earlier
whose name I forget
whichever comes first

RELATIVE PRONOUNS		
that	which	whichever
who	whoever	whose
whosoever	whom	whomever

When attaching a subordinate clause to the front of a main clause (an independent clause), it is necessary to use a comma between the two clauses.

Example:
Before I knew it, I was being lambasted by the angry sergeant for my comment.

When attaching the clause to the tail of a main clause, no comma is needed.

Example:
Put your name and number on the card **so I don't forget it.**

Practice

Determine whether the group of words is an independent or a subordinate clause.

1. It seemed like yesterday

2. Despite the fact you knew

3. If we could just see eye to eye

4. Wherever he might go

5. Before we leave

6. Suppose he changes his mind

7. Because we were only a mile from home

8. Andrew went fishing

9. When Justin took his first swing

10. So long as we remain in the boat

Subordinate clauses can function as three different parts of speech in a sentence: as a *noun*, an *adjective*, or an *adverb*.

Noun Clauses

We know that nouns can have many roles in a sentence. They can be subjects, predicate nominatives, direct objects, appositives, indirect objects, or objects of prepositions. Some words that begin noun clauses are question starters like *who, what, where, when, why, how,* as well as the words *that, whether, whom, whoever,* and *whomever.*

Example:
I see Robin.

In this sentence, the proper noun *Robin* is the direct object of the verb *see.*

Example:
I see that Robin finished three books already.

The noun clause *that Robin finished three books already* is functioning as the direct object of the verb *see.*

Example:
Charles, a local hero, received an award.

The phrase *a local hero* is an appositive phrase that modifies the noun *Charles*.

Example:

Charles, who is a local hero, received an award.

The phrase *who is a local hero* is a noun phrase functioning as an appositive.

Practice

Identify the noun clause in each of the following sentences.

11. I don't understand what he sees in this.

12. Phyllis's suggestion that we go through the Blue Ridge Mountains was a good one.

13. James was wondering what Wednesday's lineup is going to be.

14. Our intention is that we be able to visit the Eiffel Tower on our way through Paris.

15. Why you decided to switch careers this late in the game is hard to comprehend.

16. Hugh says he has no idea where he is going to sleep.

17. Whether Ursula goes to college is a concern of mine.

18. That we leave before five in the morning was her idea, not his.

19. You should know where your watch is.

20. The commendation goes to whoever accomplishes the tasks in a timely manner.

Adjective Clauses

Subordinate clauses function as adjectives when they describe or modify nouns or pronouns. Like adjectives, they answer the questions *what kind?* and *which one?* about the words they are modifying. An **adjective clause** begins with the relative pronoun *who, whose, whom, that,* or *which,* or the subordinating conjunction *where* or *when.*

Example:

The painting, which had a price tag of $10,000, was too expensive.

The adjective clause *which had a price tag of $10,000* is modifying the noun *painting.*

Example:

The man who witnessed the robbery was later interviewed by the newspaper.

The adjective clause *who witnessed the robbery* is modifying the noun *man.*

Practice

Identify the adjective clause in each sentence.

21. Did you spill the glass of milk that was in the refrigerator?

22. The police are searching for the person who lives in this apartment.

23. The room on your left is where the supervisor works.

24. Do you remember when you fell and sprained your wrist?

25. I want to go on a ride that is fast, like a roller coaster.

26. I am sure it was the car whose taillight was broken.

27. This document is a piece of evidence that is important.

28. The people whom he admires most are his parents.

29. Did the pool club that we join every year close?

30. I saw our neighbor, who teaches piano, at the opera last evening.

Adverb Clauses

When a subordinate clause answers *where, when, how,* or *why,* it is functioning as an adverb, and is called an **adverb clause**. Like other adverbs, the adverb clause will answer *where? when? why?* and *how?* about the verb, adjective, or other adverb it is modifying in the sentence. Adverb clauses begin with subordinating conjunctions such as *because, although, once, until,* and *after,* to name a few (for a complete list, see page 100).

Example:
As he set the cup down, coffee spilled all over his shoe.

The adverb clause *as he set the cup down* modifies the verb *spilled.*

Example:
Allison played the piano longer than David did.

The adverb clause *than David did* modifies the adverb *longer.*

Practice

Identify the adverb clause in each of the following sentences.

31. Because the book was old, it was kept behind glass.

32. This dining room set is yours provided that your payment goes through.

33. Mark is not allowed to leave even if he insists on going.

34. I was ready to go before the sun was up.

35. He acted as if he belonged there.

36. I enjoyed the reunion although there was some tension between Mom and Aunt Joy.

37. Tad could not reach the top shelf even though he used a stepladder.

38. The baby starts to cry whenever I step out of the room.

39. After we have breakfast, we'll go to the flea market.

40. If you don't mind, put this away in the closet for me.

▶ Answers

1. independent clause
2. subordinate clause
3. surordinate clause
4. subordinate clause
5. subordinate clause
6. independent clause
7. subordinate clause
8. independent clause
9. subordinate clause
10. subordinate clause
11. what he sees in this
12. that we go through the Blue Ridge Mountains
13. what Wednesday's lineup is going to be
14. that we be able to visit the Eiffel Tower
15. Why you decided to switch careers
16. where he is going to sleep
17. Whether Ursula goes to college
18. That we leave before five in the morning
19. where your watch is
20. whoever accomplishes the tasks
21. that was in the refrigerator
22. who lives in this apartment
23. where the supervisor works
24. when you fell and sprained your wrist
25. that is fast
26. whose taillight was broken
27. that is important
28. whom he admires most
29. that we join every year
30. who teaches piano
31. Because the book was old
32. provided that your payment goes through
33. even if he insists on going
34. before the sun was up
35. as if he belonged there
36. although there was some tension
37. even though he used a stepladder
38. whenever I step out of the room
39. After we have breakfast
40. If you don't mind

15 ▶ Conjunctions

LESSON SUMMARY

Does it matter if your connectors are *correlative*, *coordinating*, or *subordinating*, and whether the elements they are joining are similar? Find out here.

Conjunctions are connecting words. They join words, phrases, and sentences in our writing and speech. Conjunctions come in three forms: coordinating, correlative, and subordinating. Coordinating and correlative conjunctions connect elements that are similar in form: nouns with nouns, phrases with phrases, sentences with sentences. Subordinating conjunctions connect elements that are dissimilar.

▶ Coordinating Conjunctions

The acronym FANBOYS, will help you remember the seven, and *only* seven, **coordinating conjunctions**: *for, and, nor, but, or, yet,* and *so.*

COORDINATING CONJUNCTIONS	
for	expresses a logical relationship, where one element is the cause of another
Connecting sentences:	*Alice sold her condominium,* for *she wanted a house.*
and	joins elements that are equal in importance
Connecting phrases:	June *vacuumed the floors* and *dusted the furniture.*
nor	presents an alternate idea or thought
Connecting words:	He was so nervous he would neither *eat* nor *sleep.*
but	indicates a difference or exception between elements
Connecting words:	Their vacation was *short* but *enjoyable.*
or	presents an alternative or option for an element of equal importance
Connecting words:	You can have *juice* or *soda* with your meal.
yet	joins elements that follow logically but are contrary
Connecting phrases:	She is *so glamorous* yet *down to earth.*
so	suggests the consequence of related ideas
Connecting sentences:	*Marge cut the grass yesterday,* so *she got to relax today.*

Practice

In each of the following sentences, identify the coordinating conjunction and the word or group of words it is connecting.

1. The litter of puppies was calm yet noisy when I peered into the crate.

2. You or I should make sure the smoke alarm batteries are changed.

3. We took the local roads to the city for we knew the expressway would have traffic.

4. The dancer moved with great fluidity yet without passion on the stage.

5. Ken and Rona arrived early so they could get good seats for the symphony.

6. Rhonda wanted to go back to finish her degree in nursing, so she freed up three evenings a week for her classes.

7. Last week's weather was rainy, but the forecast is calling for sunny skies this week.

8. Linda was anxious, for this was her first time flying solo.

9. You may put your sweaty clothes in the basement or in the hamper, not on your floor.

10. Are these flowers annuals or perennials?

▶ Correlative Conjunctions

Correlative conjunctions come in pairs and are used as such. They connect sentence elements of similar structure and similar importance. There are five common pairs of correlative conjunctions.

CORRELATIVE CONJUNCTIONS	
both . . . and	Both Kelly and Ingrid attended the cooking demonstration.
either . . . or	Either you let him go or I'm calling the police.
neither . . . nor	I can neither go shopping nor go to the movies because the mall is closed.
not only . . . but also	We spent not only the summer but also the fall in Alaska.
whether . . . or	Sometimes I don't know whether Lynn or Jill should take the lead.

Practice

Insert acceptable correlative conjunctions into the following sentences.

11. She has _____ six _____ seven years of service with us.

12. _____ Stanley _____ Josh play drums.

13. _____ you decide on the red _____ choose the blue makes no difference to me.

14. Caroline _____ forgot where Matt lives, _____ lost his cell phone number.

15. _____ Holly will have to try harder _____ she will have to move down to a different level.

16. This lemon chiffon pie is _____ creamy _____ low-calorie.

17. _____ you call the hall to make the arrangements _____ you risk losing your $100 deposit.

18. It is unclear _____ the cable bill will come on time _____ I will have to go to the office to pay it.

19. The fee includes _____ drinks _____ gratuity at this establishment.

20. At the birthday party, Kim served _____ barbecued ribs _____ steak.

▶ Subordinating Conjunctions

Subordinating conjunctions connect an independent clause to a dependent clause (a group of words that have a subject and verb but cannot stand alone as a sentence). Dependent clauses are also called subordinate clauses. The subordinating conjunction expresses the relationship between the meanings of the independent and dependent clauses. (For a review of clauses, see Lesson 14.)

SUBORDINATING CONJUNCTIONS			
TIME	**CAUSE/EFFECT**	**CONDITION**	**CONTRAST**
after	because	as long as	although
before	so	unless	even though
when	now that	provided that	though
since	in order that	so long as	as much as
until	as if	if	while
as soon as		whether	whereas
whenever			even if

The preceding table shows some commonly used subordinating conjunctions and some relationships they convey. The logic of their use lies in the relationship of the dependent and subordinate clauses. For example, in the sentence

> The program will have to be discontinued unless more interest is generated.

the clause *unless more interest is generated* cannot stand alone because it depends for its meaning on the independent clause *The program will have to be discontinued.*

Think you're seeing things? You're not; many of the subordinating conjunctions shown above are also listed as prepositions in Lesson 9. Don't forget—words can play many different roles in a sentence! For example, depending on its sentence function, the word *since* can play three roles.

It can be an adverb:

> He's been over there since.

or a preposition:

> I haven't had fresh pineapple since my trip to Hawaii.

or a conjunction:

> We haven't been to the beach since the weather has been so unpleasant all summer.

Practice

Using the table on page 108 for reference, create a new sentence with the clauses and a subordinating conjunction.

21. Soccer is becoming popular. Baseball is all the rage.

22. The sailboat was stranded. There was not enough wind.

23. Louise will sleep soundly. Her alarm clock has gone off.

24. The horse won't get out of its stall. You lock the door.

25. Dr. Kroger has high expectations of his students. They work hard.

▶ Answers

1. calm [yet] noisy
2. You [or] I
3. We took the local roads to the city for [we] knew the expressway would have traffic.
4. with great fluidity [yet] without passion
5. Ken and Rona arrived early [so] they could get good seats for the symphony.
6. Rhonda wanted to go back to finish her degree in nursing, [so] she freed up three evenings a week for her classes.
7. Last week's weather was rainy, [but] the forecast is calling for sunny skies this week.
8. Linda was anxious, [for] this was her first time flying solo.
9. in the basement [or] in the hamper
10. annuals [or] perennials
11. either . . . or
12. both . . . and

13. whether . . . or
14. either . . . or; neither . . . nor; both . . . and
15. either . . . or
16. both . . . and; neither . . . nor
17. either . . . or
18. whether . . . or
19. neither . . . nor; either . . . or; both . . . and
20. both . . . and; neither . . . nor; either . . . or
21. *Now that* soccer is becoming popular, baseball is all the rage.
   Even though soccer is becoming popular, baseball is all the rage.
   Even though baseball is all the rage, soccer is becoming popular.
22. The sailboat was stranded *because* there was not enough wind.
   Because there was not enough wind, the sailboat was stranded.
   While there was not enough wind, the sailboat was stranded.
23. Louise will sleep soundly, *even if* her alarm clock has gone off.
   Even if her alarm clock goes off, Louise will sleep soundly.
   Louise will sleep soundly *until* her alarm clock goes off.
24. The horse won't get out of its stall *if* you lock the door.
   If you lock the door, the horse won't get out of its stall.
   After you lock the door, the horse won't get out of its stall.
25. Dr. Kroger has high expectations of his students, *as* they work hard.
   Dr. Kroger has high expectations of his students, *so long as* they work hard.
   Dr. Kroger has high expectations of his students, *so* they work hard.

Combining
Sentences

LESSON SUMMARY

Advanced writing must include sentences of varying lengths and complexity, which is achieved by combining your sentences. Learn how to do just that in this lesson.

I f you have ever read a book for young readers to a child, you may have noticed that the sentence structure is direct, simple, and short. While such language is helpful for new and emerging readers, these sentences become monotonous and uninteresting for an advanced audience. More advanced writing includes sentences of varying lengths and complexity, which are achieved by sentence combining.

Besides simple sentences, there are three other basic sentence types in writing: compound, complex, and compound-complex.

We know that independent clauses are simple sentences, which must have, minimally, a simple subject and a simple predicate. (See Lesson 11 for a review of basic sentence structure.)

Examples:

Nathan talks.
Les listens.
Nora laughs.

The following table maps out simple sentence structures with combinations of subjects, verbs, and objects. These examples do not include the infinite number of modifying words, phrases, and clauses that could be added for detail.

SIMPLE SENTENCE STRUCTURES	
(Implied subject *you*) + (**V**)erb = simple sentence	*Watch!*
(**S**)ubject + **V** = simple sentence	*Sam watched.*
S + **V** + (**O**)bject =	*Sam watched baseball.*
(**C**)ompound **S** + **V** + **O** =	*Sam and Joe watched baseball.*
S + **CV** + **O** =	*Sam watched and played baseball.*
S + **V** + **CO** =	*Sam watched baseball and football.*
CS + **CV** + **O** =	*Sam and Joe watched and played baseball.*
CS + **V** + **CO** =	*Sam and Joe watched baseball and football.*
S + **CV** + **CO** =	*Sam watched and played baseball and football.*
CS + **CV** + **CO** =	*Sam and Joe watched and played baseball and football.*

► Compound Sentences

We can combine shorter sentences into one complete thought or sentence.

Example:

Nathan, Les, and Nora enjoy talking, listening, and laughing.

While that livens the writing up a bit, it is still rather limited. To get more complex with our sentence structure, we can take two or more related sentences, or independent clauses, and join them together with the coordinating conjunction *for, and, nor, but, or, yet,* or *so,* or we can join them with a semicolon, which gives us a **compound sentence**.

Examples:

Nathan and Nora talk and laugh; Les listens.
Les listens; Nathan and Nora talk and laugh.
Nathan and Nora talk and laugh, **but** Les listens.
Les listens, **yet** Nathan and Nora talk and laugh.
Nathan and Nora talk and laugh, **so** Les listens.
Les listens, **and** Nathan and Nora talk and laugh.

The combinations are, of course, interchangeable. The coordinating conjunction *or* is a good choice in sentences where the equal subjects have an alternative, and the coordinating conjunction *nor* is a better choice where the expressions are *negative*. The conjunction *for* denotes "because," which would work grammatically, but isn't very logical.

Practice

Combine the following simple sentences to create a compound sentence.

1. Isaac went to California to visit UCLA. Isaac's parents went too.

2. I tried to cross the street. There was too much traffic.

3. The sun was shining. The weather was warm. I went to the beach.

4. Hannah looked for her lost earring. She found it under her bed.

5. It poured last night. It didn't bother us. Our party was still a blast.

6. The cat climbed the tree. It got stuck.

7. Jason had not finished the project. He put it in his briefcase.

8. We vacationed last year in Virginia Beach. We will go to Orlando this year.

9. Frank took out his fishing pole. He couldn't put bait on the hook. He didn't catch a fish.

10. I turned on my computer. I could finish my assignment. It needed to be on time.

► Complex Sentences

In addition to compound sentences, we can create **complex sentences**, by combining one independent clause and one or more subordinate (dependent) clauses.

Examples:

Les sat and listened *while Nathan and Nora laughed and talked.*
While Nathan and Nora laughed and talked, Les sat and listened.
Les sat and listened *while Nathan and Nora laughed and talked, although he wasn't feeling well.*
Although he wasn't feeling well, Les sat and listened *while Nathan and Nora laughed and talked.*

► Compound-Complex Sentences

Finally, we can create **compound-complex sentences**, using at least two independent clauses and one or more subordinate clauses.

Examples:

Les sat and listened *while Nathan and Nora laughed and talked*, **for** he wasn't feeling well.
While Nathan and Nora laughed and talked, Les sat and listened; **for** he wasn't feeling well.
Les wasn't feeling well, **so** he sat and listened *while Nathan and Nora laughed and talked*.

Note that the boldfaced word in each of these sentences is a conjunction.

Practice

Identify the independent and subordinate clauses in the following sentences and determine whether they are complex or compound-complex.

11. Karla stayed at work because she had a lot to do.

12. If we want to get to the station on time, we should hurry.

13. Although we have driven 20 miles, I have to go back home because I forgot my wallet.

14. While taking out the garbage, Tiffany tripped on a tree root and she stubbed her toe badly.

15. When Drake goes to work he has to take the New Jersey Turnpike, even if there is a lot of traffic.

16. If Jacob decides to go back to school, he will pursue his doctorate in history, although it will take more than three years for him to finish it.

17. After we arrived back home, my throat started to hurt and I became feverish.

18. Although cats are very independent pets, they will approach someone they trust for affection.

19. Sometimes computers can be obstinate, especially when they won't do what we want them to.

20. Mr. Ferrara posted the missing signs around the neighborhood, hoping that someone had seen his little dog, Jack.

► Appositive Phrases

By adding modifiers in the form of adjectives, adverbs, or phrases to any type of sentence, we can enliven it even more:

Nathan and Nora, **best friends**, talked and laughed **about last night's party**, but Les, **who wasn't feeling well**, just sat **quietly** and listened.

The appositive phrase *best friends*, the adverb phrase *about last night's party*, the noun clause *who wasn't feeling well*, and the adverb *quietly* were added to the sentences to provide more information about the subjects *Nathan, Nora, and Les*, and the predicates *laughed* and *sat*. Vivid details such as these make sentences more interesting.

▶ Answers

(Possible answers are shown.)

1. Isaac went to California to visit UCLA, **and** Isaac's parents went too.
2. I tried to cross the street, **but** there was too much traffic.
3. The sun was shining **and** the weather was warm, **so** I went to the beach.
4. Hannah looked for her lost earring; **she** found it under her bed.
5. It poured last night, **but** it didn't bother us; **our** party was still a blast.
6. The cat climbed the tree **and it** got stuck.
7. Jason had not finished the project, **yet he** put it in his briefcase.
8. We vacationed last year in Virginia Beach, **so** we will go to Orlando this year.
9. Frank took out his fishing pole, **but he** couldn't put bait on the hook, **so he** didn't catch any fish.
10. I turned on my computer **so** I could finish my assignment, **for** it needed to be on time.

(Note that in answers 11–20, the independent clauses are boldfaced and the subordinate clauses are underlined.)

11. **Karla stayed at work** because she had a lot to do. (complex)
12. If we want to get to the station on time, **we should hurry.** (complex)
13. Although we have driven 20 miles, **I have to go back home** because I forgot my wallet. (complex)
14. While taking out the garbage, **Tiffany tripped on a tree root** and **she stubbed her toe badly.** (compound-complex)
15. When Drake goes to work **he has to take the New Jersey Turnpike,** even if there is a lot of traffic. (complex)
16. If Jacob decides to go back to school, **he will pursue his doctorate in history,** although it will take more than three years for him to finish it. (complex)
17. After we arrived back home, **my throat started to hurt and I became feverish.** (compound-complex)
18. Although cats are very independent pets, **they will approach someone they trust for affection.** (complex)
19. **Sometimes computers can be obstinate,** especially when they won't do what we want them to. (complex)
20. **Mr. Ferrara posted the missing signs around the neighborhood,** hoping that someone had seen his little dog, Jack. (complex)

Punctuation

17 ▶ End Punctuation

LESSON SUMMARY

Review the basics of end punctuation and its proper placement in sentences and abbreviations.

▶ Periods

The most common form of end punctuation, the **period** (.) indicates the end of declarative sentences (statements of facts) and imperative sentences (simple commands or requests).

Examples:
Friday night is pizza night for my family.
Order an extra-large pepperoni with mushroom, please.

Periods are also used with common abbreviations, such as months, days, and measurements (e.g., Dec., Mon., 02.). Note that periods are not used for acronyms, which are abbreviations that use all capital letters (e.g., NATO, DKNY, RNA) or for postal state abbreviations (e.g., SD, AL, FL). Finally, periods are used after a person's initials (e.g., T.S. Eliot, W.C. Fields) and for name titles such as Dr., Mr., or Gov. If a sentence ends with an abbreviation that has an end period, use that period as the end mark, unless the sentence ends with an exclamation or question mark.

Example:

It happened at exactly 3 P.M.

But:

It happened at exactly 3 P.M.!

Did it happen at exactly 3 P.M.?

Practice

Insert periods in order to correctly punctuate each of the following sentences. You may check your answers against the key at the end of the lesson.

1. Mr Gerald F Kurtry is a family friend He works in St Louis

2. The 1980 eruption of Mt St Helens in Wash state destroyed more than 200 sq miles of forest and timber

3. Rep Ted Wilson commented on the property tax increases for Warren Cty residents

4. The meteor shower is supposed to begin after 12 AM Tuesday, Oct 9

5. Mr and Mrs Kuzam belong to the Elks Club of Crystal Jct, Fla

▶ Question Marks

The **question mark** (?) indicates the end of an interrogatory sentence (direct question).

Examples:

Isn't this difficult?

May I try this time?

Are you okay?

Indirect questions are really statements that only sound like questions, so they should end with a period.

Example:

She saw the frustrated look on my face and asked if she could help me. I asked her where the laundry detergent was.

▶ Exclamation Points

The **exclamation point** (!) at the end of a sentence indicates strong feeling or emotion, or authoritative or earnest commands. Interjections—free-standing words or phrases that express strong feelings—are also punctuated with an exclamation point.

Examples:

Wow! What a mess you've made!

Look where you're going!

Note: Using two or more exclamation points at the end of a sentence for extra emphasis may seem like a good idea, but in fact it's incorrect.

Practice

In each group of three, determine which sentence is properly punctuated with question marks and exclamation points.

6. a. Help! I am going to drop these groceries?
b. Help? I am going to drop these groceries!
c. Help! I am going to drop these groceries!

7. a. What did she say? I didn't hear her.
b. What did she say. I didn't hear her.
c. What did she say? I didn't hear her?

8. a. Why her? She already has two and doesn't need any more.
b. Why her! She already has two and doesn't need any more?
c. Why her? She already has two and doesn't need any more?

9. a. How shocking. I never thought she would go through with it!
b. How shocking? I never thought she would go through with it.
c. How shocking! I never thought she would go through with it!

10. a. What a great job? Can you do it again?
b. What a great job! Can you do it again?
c. What a great job. Can you do it again?

▶ Answers

1. Mr. Gerald F. Kurtry is a family friend. He works in St. Louis.
2. The 1980 eruption of Mt. St. Helens, in Wash. state, destroyed more than 200 sq. miles of forest and timber.
3. Rep. Ted Wilson commented on the property tax increases for Warren Cty. residents.
4. The meteor shower is supposed to begin after 12 A.M. Tues., Oct. 9.
5. Mr. and Mrs. Kuzam belong to the Elks Club of Crystal Jct., Fla.
6. c.
7. a.
8. a.
9. c.
10. b.

Internal Punctuation I

LESSON SUMMARY

These forms of internal punctuation can be the trickiest of all. Learn where and when it's appropriate and necessary to place these all-too-often misused marks.

▶ Commas

Commas indicate a pause in writing or speech. They are used to set apart some modifiers, phrases, and clauses, and add a sense of pacing to sentences to enhance clarity. While there are rules for comma placement, some aspects of their usage have become a matter of personal style; some writers use them more often, and others do not. Keep in mind, however, that too many or too few commas can obscure the meaning of your writing. The basic rules are simple.

Rule 1. Use commas to separate a series of three or more words, phrases, or clauses in a sentence.

Examples:

Please pick up **milk, bread,** and **bananas** from the store on your way home from work.

Shelly **grabbed her coat, put it on,** and **ran to the bus**.

However, when your item series uses the words *and* or *or* to connect them, a comma is not necessary.

Examples:

Red **and** white **and** blue are patriotic colors.

I cannot look at pictures of snakes **or** spiders **or** mice without anxiety.

Not:

Red **,** **and** white **,** **and** blue are patriotic colors.

I cannot look at pictures of snakes **, or** spiders **, or** mice without anxiety.

If you use two or more adjectives to describe a noun or pronoun in your sentence, use a comma to separate them.

Example:

He was a **happy, intelligent** child.

Be careful not to put a comma between the final adjective and the word it is modifying.

Rule 2. Set off an introductory word or phrase from the rest of the sentence with a comma. (See Lesson 13 for a review of phrases.)

Doing this helps your reader from carrying the meaning of the introduction into the main part of the sentence, which can lead to misinterpretation.

Confusing:

After eating the flower shop owner and his manager tallied the day's receipts.

It seems as though someone was very hungry . . .

Less Confusing:

After eating, the flower shop owner and his manager tallied the day's receipts.

Confusing:

Laughing Larry tried to tell the joke but just couldn't.

What a strange name, Laughing Larry . . .

Less Confusing:

Laughing, Larry tried to tell the joke but just couldn't.

A transitional phrase should also be set off by a comma if it introduces a sentence, or by two commas if it is within the sentence.

Examples:

Fluke has two eyes on its left side, and is, **in fact,** known as summer flounder.

On the other hand, winter flounder has two eyes on its right side.

Rule 3. An appositive, a word or phrase meant to rename or enhance the noun's meaning, should be set off from the rest of the sentence by commas. (See Lesson 13 for a review of phrases.)

Examples:

See, **Michael,** this is what happens when you're not careful.

Look, **Nancy,** there's the remote control.

Bangkok, **the capital city of Thailand,** is home to many beautiful Buddhist temples.

These appositive phrases set off by commas are nonrestrictive, or not essential; even if they are removed, the sentence will remain complete.

Rule 4. Use commas in dates, addresses, and in nonbusiness letter salutations and closings.

Dates

Use commas after the day of the week, the day of the month, and the year (only if the sentence continues):

> Our Barnum and Bailey Circus tickets are for Wednesday, July 18, 2007, at the Sovereign Bank Arena in New York, NY.

If you are writing only the day and month or the month and year in a sentence, no comma is necessary.

Examples:
The Barnum and Bailey Circus show was on July 18.
The Barnum and Bailey Circus show was in July 2007.

Addresses

When writing an address on an envelope or at the head of a letter, use a comma only before an apartment number and before the state abbreviation.

Example:
Marshall Grates
122 Ridge Road, Apt. 10
Ulysses Junction, MN 57231

When referring to an address within a sentence, use additional commas to substitute for line breaks.

Example:
Please send the order to Marshall Grates, 122 Ridge Road, Ulysses Junction, MN 57231.

Notice that no commas are necessary between the state and the ZIP code.

However, when alluding to a city and state in a sentence (without the ZIP code) use a comma after the state.

Example:
I traveled through St. Louis, MO, on my way to Chicago.

The same rule applies when you mention a city and country name as well:

> Sometimes Elaine travels to Paris, France, in the fall.

Salutations and Closings

When writing a letter, use a comma after the person's name and after your closing. Note that a business letter salutation requires a colon rather than a comma.

	PERSONAL LETTER	BUSINESS LETTER
Salutation	Dear Aunt Rosie,	Dear Sir/Madam:
Closing	Love,	Sincerely,
	Yours truly,	Respectfully,
	Fondly,	Best Regards,

Rule 5. Use commas before the coordinating conjunction *for, and, nor, but, or, yet,* or *so* if it is followed by an independent clause.

> **Examples:**
> Frank is retired**, and** his wife, Louise, will retire this year.
> Frank is retired**, yet** his wife, Louise, will work for another three years.

Rule 6. Use commas before, within, and after direct quotations (the exact words that a person says), whether the speaker is identified at the beginning, or at the end.

> **Examples:**
> Drew said**,** "Our trip to Aruba was awesome."
> "Our trip to Aruba," Drew said**,** "was awesome."
> "Our trip to Aruba was awesome**,**" Drew said.

Note that an indirect quote means that someone is conveying what Drew said. Do not use commas to set off the speaker in an indirect quotation.

> **Example:**
> Drew said that their trip to Aruba was awesome.

Rule 7. Commas are used with titles and degrees only when they follow the person's name.

> **Examples:**
> Arthur Mari**,** M.D.
> Sandy Dugan**,** Ph.D.
> Dr. Foster
> Dr. Sandy Dugan

Rule 8. Commas are used when writing numbers longer than three digits.

In order to make a long number like 1479363072 easier to read, it is customary to place commas after grouping numbers into threes from **right to left**, dividing them into thousands, ten-thousands, hundred-thousands, and so on: 1,479,363,072.

Exceptions to this rule are phone numbers, page numbers, ZIP codes, years, serial numbers, and house numbers.

> **Example:**
> Edison, New Jersey, has three ZIP codes: 08817**,** 08818**,** and 08820.

As in any other series, commas should be placed between whole numbers in a series of numbers.

> **Example:**
> Refer to pages 466**,** 467**,** and 468 in the phone book to find information on ZIP codes.

Practice
Add commas where necessary in the following sentences or phrases.

1. My mom lives at 521 N. Colfax Street La Habra California.

2. Thomas Jefferson died on July 4 1826 in Monticello Virginia.

3. Dear Dad

4. Very truly yours

5. February 2 2010 is our 25th anniversary.

6. Brittany's birthday party is March 21 2005 at the pavilion in West End Park in Columbia South Carolina.

7. The Blue Ridge Mountains part of the Appalachian Mountain Range begin in Georgia and run through North Carolina Tennessee Virginia and Maryland and end in Pennsylvania.

8. Vista del Gado has tacos enchiladas burritos and tostadas on their lunch menu.

9. "Just wait a minute" said Randy "and you'll see what I'm talking about."

10. Gerald Keller Ph.D. is a well-respected botanist at Princeton University.

Colons

Colons are used to introduce a word, a sentence, a list, a quotation, or a phrase. They say "here is an example" or "an example is going to follow."

Example:
On your first day of the art workshop, please bring the following items: a charcoal pencil, two paintbrushes, a drawing pad, and your creativity to room 601 of Larsson Hall.

Do not use a colon when introducing a list if the colon follows a preposition or a verb.

Incorrect:
On your first day of the art workshop, please bring: a charcoal pencil, two paintbrushes, a drawing pad, and your creativity to: room 601 of Larsson Hall.

A colon can also introduce an excerpt or long quotation in your writing,

Example:
Benjamin Franklin (1706–1790), diplomat, politician, physicist, writer, and inventor is quoted as saying: "All human situations have their inconveniences. We feel those of the present but neither see nor feel those of the future; and hence we often make troublesome changes without amendment, and frequently for the worse."

and set off the subtitle of a movie or book.

Examples:
Phenomenal Women: Four Poems Celebrating Women is written by Maya Angelou, one of America's finest female poets.
Jimmy has watched *Barnyard: The Original Party* four times this weekend.

Lastly, colons are used to separate the hour from minutes in written time,

The next bus for New York City leaves at 10:20 A.M.

and between the numbers when citing the volume and the pages of books and magazines.

Please refer to Volume 3: pages 4–9 for further information.

Semicolons

Also called the "super comma," the **semicolon** is used to link two topic-related independent clauses (sentences) together when a coordinating conjunction is not used.

Examples:

Steven's sister, Haley, is short.

Steven is tall.

Steven's sister, Haley, is short; Steven is tall.

Use a semicolon between two independent clauses joined by a coordinate conjunction (*for, and, nor, but, or, yet,* or *so*) only when commas are also used in the sentence.

Example:

Because Haley is 6′2″ tall, she is taller than most people; *but* she is the shortest sibling in her family.

Use a semicolon between two independent clauses separated by a transitional word or phrase or by a conjunctive adverb.

Example:

At 6′8″, Steven is tall; *therefore,* even at 6′2″, Steven's sister, Haley, is short in her family.

COMMON CONJUNCTIVE ADVERBS		
afterward	accordingly	besides
consequently	furthermore	hence
however	indeed	instead
likewise	moreover	nevertheless
nonetheless	otherwise	similarly
so	still	then
therefore	coincidentally	thus

Practice

Add colons and semicolons where necessary in the following sentences.

11. Darla's grocery list included six items eggs, milk, toothpaste, soap, cat food, and bleach.

12. To whom it may concern

13. Tabitha watches *Star Trek The Next Generation* after school every Tuesday.

14. Which time is better for you, 1200 P.M. or 230 P.M.?

15. Dad rang the doorbell several times he had lost his key.

16. Although Joseph is far from home, he still brings his laundry when he visits perhaps he should invest in a new washer and dryer.

17. Daren admires Winston Churchill's quote "We make a living by what we get we make a life by what we give."

18. Mr. Joe owns Kelsey's Bakery coincidentally, Kelsey owns Joe's Bar and Grill.

19. He just made a hole-in-one there was no one there to see it but him.

20. The instructions said to consult Volume J pages 30–36 and Volume P pages 89–90 for further information.

▶ Answers

1. My mom lives at 521 N. Colfax Street, La Habra, California.

2. Thomas Jefferson died on July 4, 1826, in Monticello, Virginia.

3. Dear Dad,

4. Very truly yours,

5. February 2, 2010, is our twenty-fifth anniversary.

6. Brittany's birthday party is March 21, 2005, at the pavilion in West End Park in Columbia, South Carolina.

7. The Blue Ridge Mountains, part of the Appalachian Mountain Range, begin in Georgia and run through North Carolina, Tennessee, Virginia, and Maryland, and end in Pennsylvania.

8. Vista del Gado has tacos, enchiladas, burritos, and tostadas on their lunch menu.

9. "Just wait a minute," said Randy, "and you'll see what I'm talking about."

10. Gerald Keller, Ph.D., is a well-respected botanist at Princeton University.

11. Darla's grocery list included six items: eggs, milk, toothpaste, soap, cat food, and bleach.

12. To whom it may concern:

13. Tabitha watches *Star Trek: The Next Generation* after school every Tuesday.

14. Which time is better for you, 12:00 A.M. or 2:30 P.M.?

15. Dad rang the doorbell several times; he had lost his key.

16. Although Joseph is far from home, he still brings his laundry when he visits; perhaps he should invest in a new washer and dryer.

17. Daren admires Winston Churchill's quote: "We make a living by what we get; we make a life by what we give."

18. Mr. Joe owns Kelsey's Bakery; coincidentally, Kelsey owns Joe's Bar and Grill.

19. He just made a hole-in-one; there was no one there to see it but him.

20. The instructions said to consult Volume J: pages 30–36 and Volume P: pages 89–90 for further information.

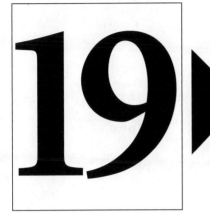

Internal Punctuation II

LESSON SUMMARY

Knowing when and how to *contract* or show *possession*, and whether to *divide*, *join*, *interrupt*, or *emphasize* your words and phrases correctly, is essential in good writing. This lesson shows you how.

Apostrophes are used to create contractions, to make nouns possessive, and in rare instances, to make a noun plural.

 Apostrophes

Contractions

Contract (con-TRACT) means to squeeze together or shorten. In speaking and in informal writing, we combine two words into one with an apostrophe, creating a **contraction**. For instance, *has* and *not* would become *hadn't*. See the following table for other common contractions.

PRONOUN CONTRACTIONS

	AM	WILL	HAVE/HAS	HAD/WOULD
I	I'm	I'll	I've	I'd
you	you're	you'll	you've	you'd
he	he's	he'll	he's	he'd
she	she's	she'll	she's	he'd
it	it's	it'll	it's	it'd
we	we're	we'll	we've	we'd
they	they're	they'll	they've	they'd

HELPING VERB CONTRACTIONS

is	+	not	=	isn't
are	+	not	=	aren't
was	+	not	=	wasn't
were	+	not	=	weren't
have	+	not	=	haven't
has	+	not	=	hasn't
had	+	not	=	hadn't
might	+	not	=	mightn't
can	+	not	=	can't
do	+	not	=	don't
did	+	not	=	didn't
should	+	not	=	shouldn't
would	+	not	=	wouldn't
could	+	not	=	couldn't

Note that the use of contractions is not acceptable in formal writing.

Possessive Nouns

Possessives are nouns that show ownership. To make a singular noun possessive, add *'s*. Be careful not to confuse the plural form of a noun with the possessive.

Plural Form:

The writer of the news **stories** won a Pulitzer.

Singular Possessive:

The news **story's** writer won a Pulitzer.

The first sentence tells us that the writer of multiple stories won a Pulitzer. The second sentence tells us that the writer of one story won a Pulitzer.

To form the possessive of the plural noun *stories*, add an apostrophe after the final *s*.

Plural Possessive:

The news **stories'** writer won a Pulitzer.

This sentence also tells us that the writer of multiple stories won a Pulitzer. The *s'* rule applies only to plural nouns ending with an *s*. For example, the possessive of the plural noun *children*, which does not end in *s*, would be children's.

To form the possessive of a singular noun ending with *s*, you can do one of two things: add *'s* or just add an apostrophe after the *s*.

Examples:

Kara Reynolds's picture was in the newspaper this morning.

Kara Reynolds' picture was in the newspaper this morning.

Plurals with Apostrophe + *s*

There are a few occasions when *'s* is required to make a noun plural.

Add *'s* to form the plural of abbreviations that contain more than one period, such Ph.D. or M.D.

Example:

M.D.'s and Ph.D.'s are doctorate degrees in medicine and philosophy.

Add *'s* to form the plural of words, letters, and numbers that we don't commonly see in the plural form.

Examples:

How many **um's** and **and-uh's** did you count in the run-through of my speech?

I got four **A's** and two **B's** on my report card.

Please write your **5's** and **8's** more clearly on tests.

Practice

Place apostrophes where they belong in the following sentences.

1. The mans rake wasnt left in the leaf pile.

2. My mothers tablecloth was stained with grease.

3. You shouldnt pull your sisters hair.

4. The secretarys phone rang off the hook all morning.

5. Maries umbrella was blown inside out.

6. The snowstorms forecast didnt keep us out of school.

7. Kyles pep talks are always the best arent they?

8. Kims team won the competition; the girls couldnt have been happier.

9. Unless the bridges rails are fixed, you may not walk on it.

10. The waitresss smile was inviting on this especially gloomy day.

► Hyphens and Dashes

Although they look similar, hyphens and dashes perform two completely different jobs in our writing; the former divide and join, while the latter interrupt and emphasize. Knowing the difference will help you better identify them in your reading and correctly utilize them in your writing.

Hyphens

Hyphens divide words at the ends of lines, separate numbers, join compound words, and attach prefixes and suffixes.

To divide a word at the end of a line of writing, place a hyphen at a syllabic break in the word.

Examples:
cir-cum-stance
ab-bre-vi-a-tion
po-ly-vi-nyl

> Syllables are the individual spoken units of a word, consisting of a vowel or a vowel-consonant combination. To find syllabic breaks in a word, simply tap your finger or clap your hand for each spoken syllable of the word. The word *syllable*, for instance, has three separate audible units: *syl*, *a*, and *ble*. To write the syllables, divide the correctly spelled word into the units you hear. (Note that not all dictionaries even agree on every spelling of all word units.)

Hyphens are used to join many prefixes, such as *great-*, *all-*, *half-*, *ex-*, *self-*, and the suffix *-elect*, to existing words in order to create a new word:

great-grandfather	great-aunt
all-encompassing	all-American
half-moon	half-hearted
ex-wife	ex-mayor
self-esteem	self-regulated
governor-elect	president-elect

Hyphens are also used to turn phrases into a single unit,

sister-in-law   jack-in-the-box   forget-me-not

to separate word units when spelling out the numbers 21 to 99 or fractions,

thirty-six   ninety-nine   six-eighths   one-fourth

and in scores and dates,

> The Red Sox beat the White Sox 10–3 on Friday.
> The article from the 08-23-06 *Chicago Sun* edition was incorrect.

Hyphens are useful to avoid confusion.

Example:
> Mr. Johnson tried to recollect how he planned to **re-collect** the student's papers this time to avoid unnecessary chaos.

They are also helpful when spelling certain compound words as one would look awkward.

Example:
> The button's shell-like appearance made it intriguing.

Without the hyphen, *shell-like* would become *shelllike*, with three *l*'s crashing together inside the word.

Dashes

Much like parentheses, **dashes** are used to indicate incidental thoughts in writing, but with a stronger emphasis.

Example:
> Louis's favorite color is—let me guess—pink!

Like a colon, but less formal, a dash can be used to set off a short series of phrases or words in a sentence.

Example:

I bought what I needed, like lipstick, blush, eye shadow, liner pencils, and foundation, at the department store cosmetic counter.

Becomes:

I bought what I needed—lipstick, blush, eye shadow, liner pencils, and foundation—at the department store cosmetic counter.

Practice

Determine where hyphens or dashes should be appropriately placed in the following sentences.

11. Everything the dresser, bed, tables, and your desk needs to be moved before we can paint.

12. At seventy nine, Mr. Perkins is extraordinarily active.

13. We made it to the top of the mountain the view was spectacular!

14. My brothers in law are the nicest guys you'd ever want to meet.

15. It is said that possession is nine tenths of the law.

16. One hundred fifty five people filed into the courthouse to view the arraignments.

17. Denny was asked to reglue the eyes onto his puppet's face, as they had fallen off.

18. Mary said her ex sister in law would always be a part of the family.

19. Jayne loves playing with her daddy's old jack in the box that her grandma brought.

20. Some old movie theme songs *M*A*S*H*, *The Pink Panther*, *2001: A Space Odyssey*, and *The Wizard of Oz* are classics that will live on for all time.

▶ Answers

1. man**'s**, wasn**'t**
2. mother**'s**
3. shouldn**'t**, sister**'s**
4. secretary**'s**
5. Marie**'s**
6. snowstorm**'s**, didn't
7. Kyle**'s**, aren't
8. Kim**'s**, couldn't
9. bridge**'s**
10. waitress**'s**
11. Everything—the dresser, bed, tables, and your desk—needs to be moved before we can paint.
12. At seventy-nine, Mr. Perkins is extraordinarily active.
13. We made it to the top of the mountain—the view was spectacular!
14. My brothers-in-law are the nicest guys you'd ever want to meet.
15. It is said that possession is nine-tenths of the law.
16. One hundred fifty-five people filed into the courthouse to view the arraignments.
17. Denny was asked to re-glue the eyes onto his puppet's face, as they had fallen off.
18. Mary said her ex-sister-in-law would always be a part of the family.
19. Jayne loves playing with her daddy's old jack-in-the-box that her grandma brought.
20. Some old movie theme songs—*M*A*S*H*, *The Pink Panther*, *2001: A Space Odyssey*, and *The Wizard of Oz*—are classics that will live on for all time.

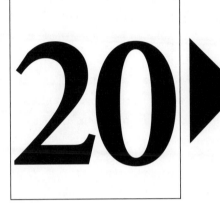

LESSON SUMMARY

It is helpful to know how to write dialogue, insert a parenthetical comment, and editorialize in your writing. Learn the proper way to go about it in this lesson.

▶ Quotation Marks

Quotation marks, or quotes, are used in writing to show the exact words that someone has said. This exact account is called a **direct quotation**. Direct quotations require the use of opening and ending quotation marks, " and ".

Example:
"Please enter your code again," the teller told Margaret patiently.

When someone *refers* to someone else's words, this is called an **indirect quotation**, which does NOT require quotation marks.

Example:

Margaret said that the teller patiently told her to please enter the code again.

Quotation marks are not used in recording someone's thoughts.

Example:

Margaret thought the teller had a lot of patience.

Putting quotation marks around a word (or words) stresses its meaning or conveys uncertainty or misgivings about its validity to the reader.

Example:

It escapes me why Victor, a Wall Street broker, was asked to speak at our Gulf Shore Lifeguard Association's meeting as an "expert" on ocean rescue techniques.

Here are some helpful guidelines for using quotation marks:

- Capitalize the first word of a direct quotation if it is the first word of the quotation or if it opens the sentence within which it is quoted.
- Always place periods and commas inside the end quotes.
- Place question marks and exclamation marks inside the end quotes only when they are part of the quotation. Otherwise, place them after the end quotes.
  Examples:
  Nancy whined, "I am so hungry!"
  Did you hear her say, "I can't eat another bite"?
- Always place colons and semicolons outside the end quote.
- Place a comma before the opening quotes when the quote is preceded by words that say or imply speaking, such as *said*, *stated*, *replied*, *cried*, and the like.
  Example:
  Cosmos whispered, "I can't see—please move over."
- When a quote is interrupted, enclose each part of the quotation in quotation marks with a comma inside the first end quotes and the interrupting words followed by a comma before the second opening quotes.
  Example:
  "The first quarter's numbers are in," remarked Ted, "and they look very encouraging!"
  Note that *and* at the beginning of the second part of the quote is not capitalized, because it is not starting a new sentence but is a continuation of Ted's first sentence.

Practice

Place quotation marks, commas, and end marks in the following sentences, and change to caps as needed, or note that they are correct as written.

1. Is this going to end soon asked Ed.

2. We want to take Dan to Ohio with us replied Rita would it be all right with you

3. Jackson said that he learned how to separate eggs at camp this summer.

4. Yes I would like that thank you said Henry

5. Isn't it just like Jane to say something like that thought Kevin

6. Your projects on photosynthesis are due on Monday said Mr. Lang

7. The police officer asked the suspect where were you on February 12 at 9:00 A.M.

8. The pictures sighed the photographer came out blurry

9. My manager reminded us that the customer is always right

10. The next stop is Chambers Street said the bus driver

▶ Parentheses

Parentheses are used to provide extra or incidental information within or at the end of a sentence. The information inside the parentheses is called a **parenthetical comment**.

Example:

Ron Kenny wound up with the Salesperson of the Year Award (remember how he struggled at the beginning of the year?).

Note that even if you can take the parenthetical comment out of the sentence, it still makes sense.

Parentheses also set off dates and page numbers within sentences, or in citations in some styles of academic writing.

Examples

Information regarding the migration of Monarch butterflies can be found in Chapter 22 (pages 97–113).

In a famous study of Jane Austen (1775–1817) and her many literary accomplishments . . . (Dawson, 1989) . . .

Parentheses can be used for itemizing numbers or letters:

Please write your (1) name, (2) address, and (3) DOB.

Please write your (a) name, (b) address, and (c) DOB.

Parentheses are also used for providing, or defining, abbreviations.

Examples:

There has been recent news from the National Aeronautics and Space Administration (NASA) . . .

The Federal Communications Commission (FCC) has issued a new . . .

Each November, the New Jersey Education Association (NJEA) holds . . .

Finally, parentheses can be used to indicate an alternative form of a written term.

Examples:

Before printing, carefully select the page(s) you need . . .

Write the name(s) on the form and submit.

Practice

Determine where the parentheses should be placed in the following sentences.

11. While at the resort, you may have breakfast a in your room, b on the deck, or c by the pool.

12. We skated or should I say swept the floor at the rink this weekend.

13. The British Broadcasting Company BBC broadcasts on cable channel 67.

14. The girls were all given brown fuzzy teddy bears cute! for their birthdays.

15. You should indicate the CDs you want before they sell out.

16. At the convenience store, there was a line that consisted of 15 people which made it not so convenient.

17. The American Automobile Association AAA has serviced millions of members since 1921.

18. On April 12, 1861, the Civil War began with the battle at Fort Sumter *National Geographic*, 2002.

19. Mohandas Mahatma Gandhi 1869–1948 was a leader of peaceful protest in India during the 1930s.

20. While fluidly interchangeable, the steps of the writing process are 1 draft, 2 write, 3 revise, 4 edit, and 5 publish.

▶ Brackets

Brackets help to clarify information, but they have a narrower range of uses than parentheses.

When you editorialize (insert your own comments within a quote), place the comment inside brackets.

Example:

Kim said, "In order for you [Katelyn] to go [to the Monmouth Mall to see a movie] you must finish the dishes first."

If the capitalization of a word in a quote needs to be altered in order to make it fit in a sentence or paragraph scheme, place the new letter in brackets.

Example:

The *New York Times* article stated that "[b]aseball, an American pastime, is favored by many women as well as children."

Note that the article would have read *"Baseball, an American pastime . . ."* in the original source.

Practice

Determine where the brackets belong in the following sentences.

21. "The Trojan Horse," stated Mrs. Mitchell, "was not a gift, but really a cleverly plotted red herring decoy created by the Greeks."

22. A favorite dance saying is that "if dance were any easier, it would be football."

23. "If I were you," said Nathan, "I wouldn't put it the project off to the last minute."

24. After my wife and I purchased it our second house, we were overjoyed.

25. "As a teacher, he Mr. Johnson is obliged to report any misconduct he sees throughout the day," said Mr. Cancro.

▶ Italics and Underlining

When writing by hand, italicizing words is difficult so we underline them instead. In printing and in word processing, we are able to use either one (although underscores are uncommon). A good rule, however, is to be consistent. Don't use one and then another in the same piece of writing.

Italicize (or underline) the titles of long works such as books, long poems, magazines, newspapers, or movies.

Examples:

James Michener's *Chesapeake*　　　　　　James Michener's <u>Chesapeake</u>
The New Yorker　　　　　　　　　　　　<u>The New Yorker</u>
Robert Frost's *Birches*　　　　　　　　　Robert Frost's <u>Birches</u>

Note that shorter works such as stories, songs, short poems, and articles are set off with quotation marks rather than italics or underline.

Italicize foreign words in your writing.

Example:

The handsome man said, "*Ciao bella*," when he left the table.

When you want to emphasize a particular word in your sentence, italicize (or underline) it. The following chart shows how emphasizing different words in a sentence can change the meaning completely.

SAME SENTENCE, FOUR DIFFERENT MEANINGS	
I like your shoes.	It is I, and only I, that like them
I *like* your shoes.	Don't love them, just like them
I like *your* shoes.	No one else's but yours
I like your *shoes*.	Not your outfit or your hair, but your shoes

Practice

Identify the words and phrases that need to be italicized (or underlined) in the following sentences.

26. "Bonjour, mon ami," my French neighbor said to me.

27. Newsweek and Time are two popular newsmagazines around the world.

28. It is so annoying when you whine—please stop!

29. Hunt for Red October is an engaging novel written by Tom Clancy, as well as a hit film.

30. How do you know it's what she wants?

▶ Answers

1. "Is this going to end soon?" asked Ed.
2. "We want to take Dan to Ohio with us," replied Rita. "Would it be all right with you?"
3. Jackson said that he learned how to separate eggs at camp this summer.
4. "Yes, I would like that, thank you," said Henry.
5. Isn't it just like Jane to say something like that, thought Kevin.
6. "Your projects on photosynthesis are due on Monday," said Mr. Lang.
7. The police officer asked the suspect, "Where were you on February 12 at 9:00 A.M.?"
8. "The pictures," sighed the photographer, "came out blurry."
9. My manager reminded us that the customer is always right.
10. "The next stop is Chambers Street," said the bus driver.
11. While at the resort, you may have breakfast (a) in your room, (b) on the deck, or (c) by the pool.
12. We skated (or should I say swept the floor) at the rink this weekend.
13. The British Broadcasting Company (BBC) broadcasts on cable channel 67.
14. The girls were all given brown fuzzy teddy bears (cute!) for their birthdays.
15. You should indicate the CD(s) you want before they sell out.
16. At the convenience store, there was a line that consisted of 15 people (which made it not so convenient).
17. The American Automobile Association (AAA) has serviced millions of members since 1921.
18. On April 12, 1861, the Civil War began with the battle at Fort Sumter (*National Geographic*, 2002).
19. Mohandas Mahatma Gandhi (1869–1948) was a leader of peaceful protest in India during the 1930s.
20. While fluidly interchangeable, the basic steps of the writing process are (1) draft, (2) write, (3) revise, (4) edit, and (5) publish.
21. "The Trojan Horse," stated Mrs. Mitchell, "was not a gift, but really a cleverly plotted red herring [decoy] created by the Greeks."

22. A favorite dance saying is that "[**i**]f dance were any easier, it would be football."

23. "If I were you," said Nathan, "I wouldn't put it [the project] off to the last minute."

24. After my wife and I purchased it [our second house], we were overjoyed.

25. "As a teacher, he [Mr. Johnson] is obliged to report any misconduct he sees throughout the day," said Mr. Cancro.

26. "*Bonjour, mon ami*," my French neighbor said to me.

27. *Newsweek* and *Time* are two popular news-magazines around the world.

28. It is *so* annoying when you whine—*please* stop!

29. *Hunt for Red October* is an engaging novel written by Tom Clancy, as well as a hit film.

30. *How* do you know it's what she wants?

How *do* you know it's what she wants?

How do *you* know it's what she wants?

How do you *know* it's what she wants?

How do you know it's *what* she wants?

How do you know it's what *she* wants?

How do you know it's what she *wants*?

Posttest

Now that you've spent a good deal of time improving your grammar skills, take this posttest to see how much you've learned. If you took the pretest at the beginning of this book, you have a good way to compare what you knew when you started the book with what you know now.

When you complete this test, grade yourself, and then compare your score with your score on the pretest. If your score now is much greater, congratulations—you've profited noticeably from your hard work. If your score shows little improvement, perhaps you should review certain chapters. Do you notice a pattern to the types of questions you got wrong? Whatever you score on this posttest, keep this book around for review and refer to it when you are unsure of a grammatical rule.

Record the answers in this book. If the book doesn't belong to you, write the numbers 1–50 on a piece of paper and write your answers there. Take as much time as you need to do this short test. When you finish, check your answers against the answer section that follows. Each answer tells you which lesson of this book teaches you about the grammatical rule in that question.

▶ Posttest

1. Circle the common nouns.

pillow	jealousy	fruit
guilt	kindness	breathe
information	clapping	mindless
FBI	cute	razor

2. Circle the abstract nouns.

knowledge	log	pleasure
deceit	pilot	jury
malice	money	banana split
carrots	warmth	hope

3. Circle the proper nouns.

Kiln	Finger	President Bush
Exxon	Jacob	Hollywood
Joyce	Florida	Greece
Jupiter	Frying Pan	NYPD

4. Circle the nouns that are pluralized correctly.

televisions	flys	mouses
womans	tooths	analyses
ferries	deers	igloos
knifes	pluses	volcanoes

5. Circle the hyphenated nouns that are spelled correctly.

jack-in-the-boxes	masses-production
runners-up	one-ways streets
dry-cleaning	X-rays

6. Circle the nouns that have been correctly made possessive.

alligator's	his's	wrists'
waitress's	my's	flowers'
puppie's	Jill's	moss'
school's	his'	schools'

7. Circle the antecedents/pronouns that properly agree in gender.

Matt/her	lizard/it
mice/they	Cheryl/she
students/it	you and I/we

8. Circle the antecedents/pronouns that properly agree in number.

kites/they	everyone/it	Paul and I/we
fishermen/they	company/it	deer/it
each/we	player/we	deer/they

9. Circle the interrogative pronouns.

where	when	who
whom	whoever	whose
how	which	whatever

10. Circle the subjective case pronouns.

We brought a goat to him as a joke.
They saw me jump into the pool after her.
She caught a cold and gave it to me.

11. Circle the objective case pronouns.

We lent it to him.
Give me a sign.
He cooked them ravioli.

12. Circle the reflexive case pronouns and underline the possessive case pronouns.

Andrew questioned himself about his decision to buy the treadmill.
His decision about buying the treadmill was rash.
Heather herself wondered what prompted him to buy it.

13. Circle the demonstrative pronoun and underline the relative pronouns.

Wasn't that the most amazing movie you've ever seen?
These are the pastries that Mr. Nichols ordered.

14. Circle the action verbs.

look	talk	help	cook
just	draw	itch	be
moisten	should	may	geranium

15. Circle the linking verbs.

take	can	now	not
never	will	are	could
would	am	how	did

16. Circle the regular verbs and underline the irregular verbs.

injure	lock	carry	write
untie	hide	mow	drive
know	grow	cost	throw

17. Circle the correct form of lay/lie in each sentence.

Sammy usually (lays, lies) his schoolbooks on his desk.

This mysterious trunk has (lain, laid) untouched in this attic for decades.

The shopkeeper (laid, lain) his apron on the counter before locking up for the night.

18. Circle the correct form of sit/set in each sentence.

Janice is (setting, sitting) the table before her guests arrive.

Jim (sat, set) down in the comfortable chair and took a short nap.

We had (set, sat) our glasses of lemonade on the orange coasters beside us.

19. Circle the correct tricky words in each sentence.

Yolanda (hanged, hung) the freshly washed shower curtain back on the bar.

I liked everything about the project (accept, except) the part where I had to give a speech.

Katelyn (can, may) run like a gazelle.

20. Identify the tense of the verbs that follow as present, past, future, present perfect, past perfect, future perfect, present progressive, past progressive, or future progressive.

am swimming	had swum
will have swum	swam
have swum	will swim
were swimming	swims

21. Circle the common adjectives in the following sentences.

Sanjay lent his laptop computer to his long-time friend Benjamin.

Soccer is the most popular sport in the world; however, Nathan prefers tennis.

Elvis was a legendary rock-and-roll performer who was loved by people everywhere.

22. Place the correct indefinite article in front of each noun.

____ hen	____ hour-long lecture
____ honorable person	____ universe
____ one-car family	____ wristwatch
____ orthodontist	____ upperclassman
____ honeybee	____ elegant dinner
____ orangutan	____ underwater city
____ ozone layer	____ opinion
____ umbrella	

23. Change the following proper nouns into proper adjectives.

Greece	Mexico	Asia
Idaho	Denmark	Hawaii
North America	Florida	France
Washington	Belgium	Vietnam
Japan	Maya	Britain

24. Determine whether the boldfaced word in each sentence is a possessive pronoun or a possessive adjective.

> I showed Charles **my** coin collection, and he told me about **his**.
> **Her** kindness was undeniable; she would always share what was **hers** with others.
> **Our** hunch was that the deed was really **theirs**, but only time would tell.

25. Determine whether the boldfaced word in each sentence is a demonstrative pronoun or a demonstrative adjective.

> **That** storm isn't moving fast enough to suit me.
> Hand me **those**, please, before you drop them.
> **This** has got to be the fastest time you've recorded yet.

26. Determine which form of comparative or superlative adjective best completes each sentence.

> The (cooler, coolest) day yet this week was Wednesday, and it was 97 degrees.
> Yuck! This rock is (slimy, slimier) than the other one.
> My shoes are the (narrower, narrowest) of all.

27. Circle the correct form of the comparative and superlative adverbs in the following sentences.

> His throat was (badder, worse) than he suspected, and it would be a while longer before he got (good, well).
> Did the homemade peach cobbler taste (good, well)?
> Of the three films, I thought that this one seemed (longer, longest).

28. Determine whether the boldfaced word in the sentence is an adjective or an adverb.

> Lori told Joe not to be too **hard** on himself.
> Living in **close** quarters can be difficult for some.
> Kyle went **straight** home after the movie.

29. Identify the prepositional phrases in the following sentences.

> Termites were found all around the building.
> Without a word, he finished dinner and went upstairs to his room.
> We drove around the back to drop off the heaviest packages first.

30. Determine whether the boldfaced word is a preposition or an adverb.

> If you spin **around** quickly, you'll probably get dizzy.
> We went out for ice cream when the show was **over**.
> She walked quickly **across** the room to see what had crashed to the floor.

31. Rewrite each sentence so that the misplaced modifiers are properly placed.

> Having been burned to a crisp, the chef threw the roast into the sink.
> Crocks of onion soup were served to the guests dripping with cheese.
> At the age of five, Kerry's parents brought her to Disney World.

32. Using the clues, write the homonyms or homographs.

> high quality/monetary penalty
> to divide/not joined together
> stumble/an excursion
> hand greeting/relinquish
> fair-minded/barely
> a rabbit/something you brush

33. Identify the simple subject in the following sentences.

Animals that sleep during the day and are awake at night are called nocturnal.

Artificial intelligence is used not only in games, but for medical purposes as well.

Please stop.

Most liked it, although some did not.

Although he lives on his own, Mike still likes coming home once in a while.

34. Identify the simple predicate in the following sentences.

Jane played hopscotch all afternoon.

Stand still, please.

We spotted a turtle on a rock nearby.

35. Identify whether the boldfaced word is a direct or an indirect object in the following sentences.

The orchestra played several Beethoven **pieces**.

The townspeople gave the **sheriff** a welcoming ovation.

The judge gave the contest **finalists** extra **time** to prepare for the last round.

36. Identify the predicate nouns and predicate adjectives in the following sentences.

On the hot summer day, Jay's turkey and mayo sandwich turned bad.

Cockatiels can become speaking birds if trained well.

Judy was a pie chef who entered and won many contests.

37. Identify the verb that correctly completes the following sentences.

Judy and Gina (try, tries) to make quilts.

Macaroni and cheese (is, are) a favorite dish of many children.

Beige or tan (are, is) the only color of pants you can wear as part of your uniform.

38. Identify the verb that will agree with the indefinite pronouns in the following sentences.

Everyone (go, goes) to the prom each year.

Something (need, needs) to be done about that leak.

While each (prefers, prefer) to eat yogurt, the time of day it's eaten varies widely.

39. Determine which pronoun best fits for proper pronoun/antecedent agreement in each sentence.

The group took _____ yearly retreat to Maine.

Everyone carefully opened _____ package.

The puppy wagged _____ tail eagerly when it saw the mailman at the door.

40. Identify the adjective and adverb phrases in the following sentences.

Some of the shoes on the far shelf cost more than $300.

The airline representative said the flight should arrive within the hour.

Even though I hung the picture up carefully, it still fell from the wall.

41. Identify the participial phrases, infinitive phrases, and gerund phrases in the following sentences.

Becoming an accomplished pianist has always been Victoria's plan.

To avoid slipping on the ice, wear boots or shoes with a ridged sole.

Leaving his entire fortune to his nephew Lewis, Zach signed his will with little trepidation.

42. Identify the appositive phrases in the following sentences.

Greg Norman, a professional golfer, is from Australia.

Maureen attends UCLA, a state university of California.

WKOR, the local weather station, forecasted rain for the next five days.

43. Determine whether each group of words is an independent or a subordinate clause.

As I said

I am learning ballroom dancing

Here are some for you

Well, if you say so

That's life

Stop that

44. Identify the adjective clause in each sentence.

I sang a song that my mom sang to me when I was a baby.

The boy at the end of the line closed the door.

The Asian market where they sell many exotic fruits is down the road from us.

45. Identify the noun clause in each sentence.

I know that drinking water is better than drinking soda.

Do you know what time the store opens?

I can't decide which shoes to wear.

46. Identify the adverb clause in each sentence.

Except for Tanya, we all got soaked while walking back from the auditorium.

Whether or not you believe it, the decision is ultimately yours.

Violet decided to go home for the holidays since her grandparents would be visiting, too.

47. Identify the coordinating conjunctions in each sentence, and the word or group of words it is connecting.

Gold or blue would be the best choice of color for the pillows.

Danielle and Joanna watched a movie, popped popcorn, and stayed up all night talking.

Sometimes we go to the lake so we can water-ski.

48. Identify the simple, compound, complex, and compound-complex sentences.

a. Some citizens voted in the town election, but many did not.

b. To make mashed potatoes, just add butter and milk to the boiled potatoes and mash until creamy.

c. Put your folded laundry away, please.

d. Because Jill was late, she missed the introductory overview of the entire workshop.

49. Add punctuation where necessary in the following sentences.

On April 12 1861 the Civil War began with the battle at Fort Sumter

The dentists hygienists and staff threw a surprise party for him

Would you consider using Benjis or Jesss racket for now

50. Correctly place quotation marks, commas, and end marks in the following sentences.

It's not easy to memorize all of the mathematical formulae for algebra stated Mrs. Shapiro, but we'll accomplish that by the year's end

Would you make my steak sandwich without onions please asked Harry

I began Courtney am not the only girl who feels that way

▶ Answers

If you miss any of the following questions, you may refer to the designated lesson for further explanation.

1. pillow, fruit, information, razor (Lesson 1)

2. knowledge, pleasure, deceit, malice, hope (Lesson 1)

3. President Bush, Exxon, Jacob, Hollywood, Joyce, Florida, Greece, Jupiter, NYPD (Lesson 1)

4. televisions, analyses, ferries, igloos, pluses, volcanoes (Lesson 2)

5. jack-in-the-boxes; runners-up, dry-cleaning, X-rays (Lesson 2)

6. alligator's, wrists', waitress's, flowers', Jill's, school's, schools' (Lesson 2)

7. lizard/it, mice/they, Cheryl/she, you and I/we (Lesson 3)

8. kites/they, Paul and I/we, fishermen/they, company/it, deer/it, deer/they (Lesson 3)

9. who, whom, whoever, whose, which (Lesson 3)

10. We brought a goat to him as a joke.
They saw me jump into the pool after her.
She caught a cold and gave it to me.
(Lesson 3)

11. We lent it to him.
Give me a sign.
He cooked them ravioli.
(Lesson 3)

12. Andrew questioned himself about his decision to buy the treadmill.
His decision about buying the treadmill was rash.
Heather herself wondered what prompted him to buy it.
(Lesson 3)

13. Wasn't that the most amazing movie you've ever seen?
These are the pastries that Mr. Nichols ordered.
(Lesson 3)

14. look, talk, help, cook, draw, itch, moisten (Lesson 4)

15. can, will, are, could, would, am, how, did (Lesson 4)

16. injure   lock   carry   write
untie   hide   mow   drive
know   grow   cost   throw
(Lesson 5)

17. lays, lain, laid (Lesson 5)

18. setting, sat, set (Lesson 5)

19. hung, except, can (Lesson 5)

20. **am swimming:** present progressive
had swum: past perfect
will have swum: future perfect
swam: past
have swum: present perfect
will swim: future
were swimming: past progressive
swims: present
(Lesson 6)

21. laptop; longtime; popular; legendary; rock-and-roll (Lesson 7)

22. a hen, an honorable person, a one-car family, an orthodontist, a honeybee, an orangutan, an ozone layer, an umbrella, an hour-long lecture, a universe, a wristwatch, an upperclassman, an elegant dinner, an underwater city, an opinion (Lesson 7)

23. Greek, Mexican, Asian, Idahoan, Danish, Hawaiian, North American, Floridian, French, Washingtonian, Belgian, Vietnamese, Japanese, Mayan, British (Lesson 7)

24. **my:** possessive adjective; **his:** possessive pronoun
Her: possessive adjective; **hers:** possessive pronoun
Our: possessive adjective; **theirs:** possessive pronoun
(Lesson 7)

25. **That:** demonstrative adjective
those: demonstrative pronoun
This: demonstrative pronoun
(Lesson 7)

26. coolest; slimier; narrowest (Lesson 7)

27. worse, well; good; longest (Lesson 8)

28. **hard:** adverb; **close:** adjective; **straight:** adverb (Lessons 7 and 8)

29. around the building; Without a word; to his room; around the back (Lesson 9)

30. **around:** adverb; **over:** adverb; **across the room:** preposition (Lesson 9)

31. The chef threw the roast, which was burned to a crisp, into the sink.

Crocks of onion soup dripping with cheese were served to the guests.

When Kerry was five, her parents brought her to Disney World.

(Lesson 10)

32. fine/fine   wave/waive

separate/separate   just/just

trip/trip   hare/hair

(Lesson 10)

33. Animals; Artificial intelligence; (you); Most; Mike (Lesson 11)

34. played; stand; spotted (Lesson 11)

35. **pieces:** direct object; **sheriff:** indirect object; **ovation:** direct object; **finalists:** indirect object; **time:** direct object (Lesson 11)

36. **bad:** predicate adjective; **birds:** predicate noun; **chef:** predicate noun (Lesson 11)

37. try; is; is (Lesson 12)

38. goes; needs; prefers (Lesson 12)

39. its; his or her; its (Lesson 12)

40. **of the shoes:** adjective phrase; **on the far shelf:** adverb phrase; **within the hour:** adverb phrase; **from the wall:** adverb phrase (Lesson 13)

41. **Becoming an accomplished pianist:** gerund phrase

To avoid slipping on the ice: infinitive phrase

Leaving his entire fortune to his nephew Lewis: participial phrase

(Lesson 13)

42. a professional golfer

a state university of California

the local weather station

(Lesson 13)

43. **As I said:** subordinate

I am learning ballroom dancing: independent

Here are some for you: independent

Well, if you say so: independent

That's life: independent

Stop that: independent

(Lesson 14)

44. that my mom sang

at the end of the line

where they sell many exotic fruits

(Lesson 14)

45. that drinking water is better than drinking soda

what time the store opens

which shoes to wear

(Lesson 14)

46. Except for Tanya

Whether or not you believe it

since her grandparents would be visiting, too

(Lesson 14)

47. Gold **or** blue

Danielle **and** Joanna; watched a movie, popped popcorn, **and** stayed up all night talking

Sometimes we go to the lake **so** we can water-ski.

(Lesson 15)

48. **a.** compound; **b.** compound-complex; **c.** simple; **d.** complex (Lesson 16)

49. On April 12, 1861, the Civil War began with the battle at Fort Sumter.

The dentist's hygienists and staff threw a surprise party for him.

Would you consider using Benji's or Jess's racket for now?

(Lessons 17–20)

50. "It's not easy to memorize all of the mathematical formulae for algebra," stated Mrs. Shapiro, "but we'll accomplish that by the year's end."

"Would you make my steak sandwich without onions, please?" asked Harry.

"I," began Courtney, "am not the only girl who feels that way."

(Lessons 17–20)